INVEST IN LIVING

HOME DECORATING

by

R.W. DRAYCON

EP Publishing Limited
1977

The *Invest in Living* Series

About the Author

Roy Draycon has devoted a long professional career to many aspects of design, craftwork and both internal and external decoration and restoration. While in the service of the Home Office for seventeen years, he organised courses in Painting and Decorating in Youth Training Establishments. Later he worked on the Schools Council's Design Education Project as an Honorary Research Fellow at the University of Keele.

He is a Fellow of the College of Craft Education and from 1968 to 1972, while in the service of the Inner London Education Authority, acted in an advisory capacity in Craft and Technical projects.

More recently, while in the service of the Northamptonshire County Council, he worked with young adolescent students on the conversion of obsolete double-decker buses into mobile play schools for the under-fives. While with the same authority he produced, with other groups of senior boys and girls, a teaching film on Home Decorating which is now widely used in Upper Schools and Colleges of Further Education.

Roy Draycon is particularly interested in all aspects of design in the home and in the problems of young people setting up home for the first time.

The publishers wish to acknowledge the help of the following in providing cover photographs: Crown Decorative Products Ltd, Marshall Cavendish Ltd/Photo: N. Hargreaves and ICI Ltd.

Copyright © EP Publishing Ltd 1977

ISBN 0 7158 0462 6

Published 1977 by EP Publishing Ltd, East Ardsley, Wakefield, West Yorkshire WF3 2JN

Printed and bound in Brighton England by G. Beard & Son Ltd

Contents

Introduction

Home ownership is the ultimate ambition of most people. In the past the achievement of this ambition has largely been the aim exclusively of married couples, but today more and more single people, of both sexes, are buying properties as an investment. We are in an age when it would seem that bricks and mortar are the soundest options open to investors since houses tend, at least, to keep pace in value with the rate of inflation. All else, including money itself, no matter how it is invested, suffers from the current instability of world monetary values. Additionally, the house provides the fundamental necessity of shelter, so that it becomes a double asset.

The earlier one can make the house purchase, the easier are the loan repayments since the mortgage can be spread over a maximum period, thus reducing the amount of the monthly repayments. House purchase early in life usually means, however, that the instalments represent a high proportion of the salaries earned by the young people buying the house, thus leaving minimal margins of cash for the essential maintenance and upkeep of the property, particularly as rates are spiralling upwards at an alarming speed. It becomes, therefore, virtually essential for the young house purchaser to resort to 'Do-it-Yourself' upkeep and maintenance of his property, be it new and modern in type or of older, pre-war vintage.

Repairs and redecoration have, like all services, rocketed in cost in recent years and there is little sign that these steep increases will tail off in the foreseeable future. The advent of VAT has increased the cost of labour charges to add to the financial burden, so that 'self-help' is the order of the day for most of us. To neglect essential repairs and decoration is to undermine the whole investment and, in the end, may be the cause of extensive damage beyond the skill and ability of the DIY owner to repair, thus making it necessary to call in a professional repairer, whose resulting bill will be even higher than it would have been if his services had been sought in the first place.

Prevention, particularly in the field of property, is far less expensive than cure, and it is at the prevention level that the DIY enthusiast comes into his own. Enthusiasm, however, is not enough in itself. It is the object of this book to help the self-help owner to assess what he himself can tackle and what must, essentially, be left to the expert. Much damage can be caused by acting on 'a little learning', and the well-intentioned enthusiast will be well advised to weigh up, honestly and carefully, just what he can reasonably and successfully undertake.

Modern materials and tools go a long way towards making the work of the non-professional easier. Non-drip paints, self-adhesive vinyl wall coverings, easily handled, clean adhesives, good fillers and reasonably inexpensive, portable electric tools such as jig-saws, rotary and orbital sanders, and multi-purpose drills, all contribute to the increased ease with which home maintenance can be undertaken by the determined amateur.

The modern Upper Schools, almost without exception, provide courses for both boys and girls in Home Maintenance and Decoration, so that we are breeding and educating a generation of young people, who will think nothing of taking on the decoration of their homes, of tackling minor repairs and carrying out the redesigning and layout of kitchens, bathrooms, etc. For older people, less fortunate in this respect, there are evening courses on repairs and decorating in the home at most Evening Institutes, and one evening per week given up to the pursuit of such money-saving activities pays exceptionally good dividends: practice makes perfect.

The best time to tackle routine redecoration is before too much repair and basic preparation become necessary. Internal decorating can be undertaken at any time of the year, though clearly the long, light evenings of spring, summer and early autumn are the best. For outside activity one should certainly choose the warmest, driest three months of the year so that woodwork is as dry as it will ever be, because any attempt to paint over damp surfaces is a certain recipe for early failure of the paint film and further deterioration of the wood structure. Surfaces painted towards the end of the day may be ruined by heavy dew overnight, so that early spring and late autumn painting is to be avoided on outside work.

One last piece of general advice: always buy the best materials and tools that you can afford. This is not necessarily consistent with the highest prices charged. End-of-season offers and sale reductions and end-of-production-line bargains can often provide the sort of opportunity which will enable the watchful enthusiast to use better materials and tools than he could otherwise afford. 'Shop around' is sound, economic advice. Preparation, cleanliness, method and a relaxed approach all pay exceptional dividends in the pursuit of home decorating—try to avoid too rigid a time schedule. Who knows! You may find the work rewarding and fascinating to such an extent that you, too, become an enthusiast.

1 · Pre~planning

Making sure the structure is sound. Choosing the most suitable media and materials for existing conditions. Estimating the time required to decorate a room.

Assessing the basic structure

Before deciding on the final appearance required, it is essential that a hard, realistic appraisal is made of what is required to achieve that end. Obviously the requirements will vary widely for an old, pre-war house and a modern, recently built home. It is not only the simple age differential that has to be taken into consideration. Over the years, for a variety of reasons, building techniques have changed very considerably, and many of the materials now in common use can be quite different from those widely used 30 to 40 years ago. Seldom, for example, do we now find the floor of a ground floor room constructed of wood; partitions between rooms are often no more than particle boarding instead of the once universal breeze blocks or, even earlier, bricks. Ceilings are no longer constructed of lath and plaster and few internal doors are framed and panelled.

Cavity walls are now found everywhere and problems arising from damp are of a different order from those found in older houses without this provision. It is damp that, very frequently, is a major cause of the early deterioration of both internal and external decoration leading, all too frequently, to structural damage. In recent years it has become increasingly difficult to obtain well-seasoned timber, and this has led to warping, shrinking and splitting in doors, fitments, and even roof structures. Against this, many modern fitments go a long way towards eliminating the need for frequent decorating and replacement. One striking example of this is the way

that plastic is now almost always used for guttering and plumbing accessories of all types. The use of this material reduces the need for replacement to the occasional structural damage rather than any deterioration through rust and erosion. Plastics can be made self-colouring, thus requiring no periodic repainting. Joints in plastic accessories are, however, subject to leaking if badly fitted and this can lead to subsequent dampness and to ultimate structural damage to facia boards, walls, fitments, etc.

Most well-established manufacturers of paints, adhesives, fillers, wall coverings and accessories have kept pace with modern building techniques and now market materials and fitments suited to modern conditions and to use by DIY operators with only a minimum of practical experience.

If the pre-planning of your activities includes, for example, the redesigning of the kitchen, it is essential that light direction, ventilation, plumbing and power supply points be most carefully considered. Unless you are the exception, and are qualified to do so, do not attempt to redirect water, gas or electric supplies yourself. You will find it cheaper in the long run to consult your local plumber, gas or electrical engineers. Get an estimate for the job before making any final decisions —you may well change your mind about any fundamental changes when you learn the cost! Much can be achieved without far-reaching changes and the average practical man or woman can replace old-fashioned taps, sink units and lighting fixtures, if care is taken. Practical assistance on these aspects of the work can be obtained from other books to appear in this series.

Before commencing work, locate any sources of dampness, either from natural sources such as rain and condensation, or from leaks from plumbing installations, pipes and gutters, and eradicate these completely before proceeding with your decoration. Sometimes, particularly in older houses, eradication of these particular troubles can be frustrating and difficult as there is often no adequate damp-proof course or cavity wall construction. There are now, however, on the market several types of protective coverings which help to eliminate the effect of dampness, though even the best of these must be regarded as no more than a palliative. Wherever possible, the source of the trouble must be located and eliminated although this may, in some cases, be a costly business involving the employment of a competent professional builder.

In the more modern house, you may be assured that a good damp-proof course is incorporated in your external walls and such dampness as appears can usually be traced to poor sealing of joints, etc., and to the severe deterioration of surface protection. The former may be eliminated by using one of the efficient, modern mastics (see p. 10), while the latter may be restored by stripping and re-surfacing with the appropriate material. Evidence of skimped workmanship, the result of an effort to keep down prices, may quite often be seen—poor sealing, inadequate painting, hasty fitting, even damaged components. Time and patient application are usually all that are needed to remedy these potentially expensive faults, and the conscientious owner will have his time and labour well repaid if he assiduously attends to these points before spending more time and precious money on redecorating, either internally or externally.

Choosing materials to suit your needs

Having eliminated possible sources of structural deterioration, it will then be time to turn your attention to the best materials to use for the decorating of your home. The market is now very wide and the choice of materials considerable. For external use, there exist mould-deterrent finishes, sealers, salt-resistant paints, non-drip gloss, eggshell, flat and emulsion paints (see Glossary). There are special Portland Cement paints for masonry walls to protect the surface against the ingress of moisture.

Internally, you have the choice of painted or covered walls, but here again you need to consider carefully the use to which the room is subjected. Bathrooms and kitchens will require a covering that is impervious to heat, moisture and grease spots, and one that is easily cleaned by routine washing without harm to the surface (see Chapters 3 and 6). Rooms to be used by children need to be kept clean easily of finger-marks, yet be resistant to knocks from toys, trolleys and so on.

The question of light has to be considered. Some rooms are badly designed as far as light is concerned; choosing the correct covering can help here. The surface finish of ceilings and walls may dictate a particular type of finish. Poorly finished surfaces may be quite unsuitable for painting without a great deal of work being done on them. In cases of this sort, paper, vinyl or fabric wall coverings are more likely to give a satisfactory 'finish'.

Buying paint or paper—always buy enough

When you have considered all these points, it will be time for you to prepare your room and purchase your materials. If you intend to use a wall covering, paper, vinyl or fabric, always be sure to purchase enough (see pp. 42–4). Nothing is more annoying than finding that you are one roll short and your supplier has sold the last roll since you purchased yours. New stocks may not quite match with those that you have, or the particular design that you have chosen may be discontinued. It is far better to have a little in hand than to be short—you may well find that it comes in handy for patching up damage at a later date. The same principle applies if you have chosen to paint your walls. Even tins which nominally contain paint of the same colour, may vary from batch to batch; any honest supplier will certainly tell you as much. See p. 25.

Estimating the time required

Part of your planning will, of course, include an estimate of the time that it will take you. Can you complete the job in one day? A weekend? Or will you have to wait until you have a week's holiday? It is, of course, virtually impossible to give a precise timetable for general application, since no two jobs present precisely the same problems, but a rough guide to help you is given on the basis of a typical room, measuring 4.5 m × 3.5 m × 2.5 m high ($14\frac{3}{4}$ ft. × $11\frac{1}{2}$ ft. × $8\frac{1}{4}$ ft.). The room contains one flat door and one french window, 2 m × 2 m (6 ft. 6 in. × 6 ft. 6in.). Let us say that you intend to put emulsion paint on the ceiling, a vinyl wall covering on all the walls, which are in average condition, and for which you need eight rolls (see p. 43), and you will paint all 'trim'. You do not, on this occasion, plan to do any work on the floor. Working without undue hurry, the following is a profitable timetable:

	Hours
Washing ceiling, walls and woodwork	4
Sizing walls	1
Filling cracks, making good damaged areas and rubbing down	2
Giving two coats of emulsion paint to ceiling	3
Painting doors, french windows and skirting, two coats ..	9
Hanging wall covering, using traditional pasting methods ..	12
Total time ..	31

From this example you can get a fair idea of the time you would take on a larger or smaller room; more doors and windows and preparing walls in better or worse conditions would all affect the time schedule. Allow rather more time for panelled doors (say, 50 per cent) and dormer type rooms (25 per cent), and if you plan to paper your ceiling before applying emulsion paint, add a further 3–4 hours.

Before starting, make sure that you have purchased, hired or borrowed all the necessary accessories, equipment and tools. A list of what you will need is on pp. 12–3. The methodical pre-planning of your work will more than repay the time and thought expended on such foresight. Now move on to Chapter 2 for the basis of a successful conclusion to your decorating, namely, the restoration of surface blemishes and structural damage and the general preparation of the room.

2 · Preparations

Restoration of surface blemishes and structural damage, externally and internally. Elimination of the effects of damp, rot, woodworm, etc. A comprehensive kit for home decorating. Safety factors.

All time, effort and money spent on your decorating will almost certainly be wasted unless you are scrupulously thorough in your preparation of all surfaces to be treated.

External preparation

Externally, all physical damage to the surface must be carefully repaired, holes filled, rotted timbers replaced and all necessary pointing to walls and brickwork carried out.

Cleaning

All loose plaster, cement and paint must be removed by brushing with a stiff wire brush. The surface should then be washed but, if the area to be treated is particularly dirty, you should scrub it thoroughly with warm water to which trisodium phosphate has been added. Any good hardware store or paint shop will sell you a proprietary brand of trisodium phosphate, usually in dry powder form in packets: follow carefully the instructions on the packet. Thorough rinsing should follow and the surface be allowed to dry completely.

Fillers for woodwork

For woodwork, putty or one of the many proprietary fillers on the market should be used, but where any movement is possible or where expansion and contraction are likely, you should use one of the flexible fillers available from hardware stores and caravan distributors. These are usually supplied in tubes which are easily handled and are supplied with a nozzle that facilitates application of the filler along cracks and joints. Care should be taken to see that the space is completely filled and that a surplus of filler is left proud of (i.e. raised above) the surface. Practically all fillers contract after drying out and any surplus of hard-set filler can be glass-papered flat. Glass-paper for this purpose may be obtained in single sheets and grades 0 (fine), 1 (medium) and M2 (coarse) are best for this job.

New or porous walls

It is always best to go over porous or new walls with a coat of sealer (see pp. 16–7), before applying the final finish. In damp or shaded areas a mould-resistant base paint should be used. Remember, two or more thin coats, evenly applied, are far better than one thick one.

Removing old paint

Old paint on external woodwork should be burnt off with a blow-lamp. This may be done with the traditional paraffin blow-lamps or with one of the modern, easily handled, propane or butane liquid gas blow-lamps. The latter are clean, convenient and less expensive to purchase in the first place, but are a little more expensive operationally. Used in conjunction with either type of blow-lamp will be stripping knives and a shave hook to remove the paint made flexible by the heat from the blow-lamp. The blow-lamp should be used in such a way that the flame does not burn the woodwork but merely renders the paint flexible. It should

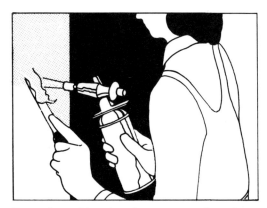

Removing old paint from external surfaces with a blow-lamp and stripping knife. Adjust the flame and speed of working so that the paint film softens and blisters away from the woodwork. At this point remove the softened paint with your stripping knife. Take particular care around window frames and glazed doors since you will crack the glass if you bring the flame too close to it. Try to scorch the wood as little as possible since paint will not adhere to heavily scorched wood

be noted that a little scorching of the surface of the wood is inevitable. The prudent amateur will practise this operation on an old, unimportant painted surface until he acquires the knack.

Internal preparation

Removing old paper

Much of what has been said about external preparation applies to internal work. Firstly, any residual wall covering in the form of paper, vinyl or fabric must be removed. If the previous covering has been a vinyl, foil or fabric product (see p. 41), it may be easily removed by lifting one corner of the covering and then pulling the vinyl, foil or fabric from the base paper. If the wall is in good condition, the base paper may be left on and used as a lining paper for the new covering. It should be mentioned here that joints in any subsequent wall covering should be so arranged as not to coincide with the joints on the base paper.

Should it for any reason be necessary to remove the base paper, it may be stripped off in the same way as standard wallpaper, i.e. by soaking with warm water, using a sponge and then stripping the paper off with a stripping knife. This procedure will have to be followed if it is proposed to replace a wall covering with paint.

Filling and sizing

Any cracks, holes, etc., should then be filled with a proprietary internal filler, left proud and, when dry, glass-papered flat as previously described. New walls, or walls that have had paper wetted and scraped off, should be 'sized' before re-covering. Size consists of well-diluted adhesive. This closes the 'pores' of the plaster wall, helps subsequent adhesion and allows the covering to be slid easily into position.

Preparing paintwork

The preparation of paintwork is quite similar to that for external painting except that it is not usually necessary to burn off the old paint with a blow-lamp. The use of graded glass-paper is normally all that is required to remove old, loose paint, to smooth out irregularities and to provide a 'key' for the new paint. If the old paint is in a very bad state, use first coarse grade, then medium, then fine. Any new wood used in the repair or 'making good' of fitments, skirting boards, doors, window-frames, and so on, should have a first coat of wood primer before you apply an undercoat or gloss paint.

Sanding floors

If the floors of an older house are to be painted or stained and varnished, or if wood blocks are to be fitted, then it will almost certainly be necessary to inspect them very closely. Years of wear, drying out and natural shrinkage will in all probability result in the knots standing out, causing an irregular and uneven surface.

This would show up badly when painted or varnished and would make the laying of blocks quite impossible. To restore the floor to a truly plane, flat surface, it will be necessary to 'sand' it. This is best achieved by the use of a large rotary commercial sander. These may, conveniently and reasonably cheaply, be hired by the day or half-day from a local hire firm. If you are unable to trace a hire firm in the Yellow Pages, then any good paint and wallpaper stockist or DIY store will be able to put you in touch with one. These large rotary sanders will do the job quickly, easily and far more efficiently than any other method.

Dealing with damp

Any area of damp must be carefully inspected and the source traced. Make certain, outside the house, that soil or rubbish has not built up above the damp-proof course or that blocked drains or ventilators are not the cause of the trouble; these are quite common causes of dampness and the cure is obvious and easy to effect. In older buildings it may be necessary to coat suspect surfaces with mould-resistant damp-proof sealer (see Chapter 3). Unfortunately, such treatment will probably only effect a temporary improvement and may require frequent inspection and repeated treatment. Sometimes a coat of Portland Cement paint (see p. 35) is more effective over a longer period but the root cause, in older houses, lies in the construction and may prove very costly to eradicate entirely.

Dealing with woodworm

Where any signs of woodworm appear, treat this very seriously as its effects can spread very rapidly, causing considerable damage, possibly to some basic structures. This could lead to heavy bills for a professional builder's attention. A sure and effective remedy for a mild attack in obvious places is to paint the affected areas with a fifty-fifty solution of paraffin and turpentine or white spirit. After several applications of this mixture you should have no more trouble from this source. Where the effects of woodworm are extensive, remove all affected wood and have it replaced with new. To be on the safe side, have all the adjacent structural woodwork treated by a professional firm of Pest Exterminators. This will be cheaper in the long run than the bill you could receive for repairs to affected structures.

Home decorating kit

Having now carefully prepared the area to be decorated, internally and/or externally, you must give some thought to the tools and equipment that you will be needing. Assuming that it will be necessary for you to decorate your home, or homes, over a period of 30 to 40 years, you will be well advised to invest in the following:
- a three-fold extending aluminium ladder. This should be sufficiently long to reach, with ease, the highest areas to be painted or repaired. Alternatively, such ladders may be hired by the day from a local firm, probably the same one from which you may have hired your rotary sander. You will, however, more than pay for the ladder after three or four hirings
- 2 pairs of step ladders, about 2 m (6 ft.) in maximum height. Alternatively, buy one pair and try borrowing a second pair from your neighbour on the understanding that you will be glad to return the favour at any time
- 1 builders' board (a plank for standing on), approximately 2.5 m × 250 mm × 40 mm (8 ft. × 9 in. × $1\frac{1}{2}$ in.). You can usually pick up one of these cheaply from a builders' yard
- 1 set of good quality paint-brushes: 100 mm (4 in.), 75 mm (3 in.), 50 mm (2 in.), 25 mm (1 in.), 13 mm ($\frac{1}{2}$ in.). If you have fitted radiators, equip

Part of a home decorating kit: **a** — filling knife, **b** — stripping knife, **c** — shave hook, **d** — scraper, **e** — hammer and pin punch, **f** — wire brush, **g** — Stanley knife, **h** — blow-lamp (liquid gas)

yourself with a special 'radiator brush' for getting into those awkward places (see p. 58)

- 1 set of rollers with tray (see p. 19); 1 set of paint pads
- 1 hammer (medium weight, 340–450 g [12–16 oz.]) and 1 pin punch
- 1 stripping knife, 1 filling knife, 1 shave hook

- 1 wire brush; 2 packets of wire wool (1 coarse, 1 medium)
- 1 folding paste table (unnecessary if you intend to use only self-pasting coverings)
- 1 100 mm (4 in.) pasting brush (again, may be unnecessary)
- 1 smoothing-out brush (for brushing down coverings when applied to the

walls and for brushing out air bubbles)
- 1 pair of 200 mm (8 in.) shears (scissors)
- 1 plumb-bob and line, some chalk
- 1 trimming knife (a Stanley knife)
- 1 joint roller
- 1 sponge; 1 bucket
- glass-paper, grades 0, 1 and M2
- emery cloth, grades fine, medium and coarse
- 2 plastic paint-pots with handles
- cover sheets.

The above list shows the minimum requirements for a comprehensive kit for home decorating. You may also wish to use a spray gun (see p. 20). These are quite expensive, and unless you intend to do a great deal of spray work over an extended period, you would be well advised to explore the cost of hiring a set of spray gun and compressor for the duration of your work. You may well offset some of the expense involved by the more economical use of paint and by the time saved by spraying.

You may not wish to use wall coverings that require pasting, preferring to paint all of your surfaces or to use one of the pre-pasted papers or those that require the wall to be pasted, not the covering. In either case, you can dispense with the folding paste table. It is possible to use the kitchen table for pasting the paper but these are usually shorter and wider than a proper pasting table and render the job of pasting and folding much more difficult and frustrating—the small outlay on a true pasting table is well worth while.

Safety first

Statistics show that there are more accidents in the home than on the roads and many of these occur during painting and decorating. Mostly they could be avoided with greater care and proper preparation. You will see, from the above recommended list, that two pairs of steps are recommended. These, used in conjunction with the builders' board, offer a sound, firm scaffold on which to paint or paper in high places, enabling the operator to move over a reasonably wide area in safety. The board is placed between the steps at a height convenient to the decorator, comfort and ease of movement being the deciding factors.

As far as possible, the room should be cleared of all obstacles and obstructions, such as furniture, pictures, mirrors, book-shelves. The floor, in particular, should be free of all obstructions with the carpets taken up and all mats removed. The floor and any furniture or fitments that cannot be removed should be covered with the sheets prescribed in the recommended list of kit. To avoid accidental damage while working, the windows, from which all curtains or blinds should have been removed, should be painted over with whitewash so that they are instantly visible. Lampshades should be removed but, as a safety precaution, the bulbs should be left in the fittings.

Cleaning equipment

For the ultimate cleansing of brushes, rollers and pads, it will be necessary to provide a bucket, some large tins and some turpentine or white spirit if one of the older types of gloss paint has been used (modern gloss paints from good companies only require that the brushes be washed out in warm water to which a little detergent has been added). If polyurethane paints or varnish have been used, it is advisable to use the recommended thinners to wash out the brushes since they will go rock-hard if left for only a few minutes.

Copious supplies of old newspapers will prove very helpful if you are using wall coverings that have to be pasted—they make for cleanliness all round.

Having made all the necessary preparations, you can now turn to Chapter 3 for help with your painting.

3 · Painting (i)

Types of paint for different surfaces—suitability, range and colour. Basic equipment. How to estimate quantity required, time and cost.

As outlined in Chapter 1, there are at our disposal a very wide range of paints from a number of reputable manufacturers. Years of research and developments have resulted in a very sophisticated technology in the field of paints and you need to assess very carefully your specific needs. It may be helpful to outline, in some detail, some of the more widely used paints, so that your final choice suits perfectly your own particular needs. For the amateur decorator, paints may be conveniently divided into six categories:

1. Paints for woodwork
2. Paints for metals
3. Paints for masonry, concrete, brickwork and plaster
4. Paints for building boards, sheets, slabs and papered surfaces
5. Paints for floors
6. Paints for use in exceptional conditions and circumstances

Paints for woodwork

Wood primers are low lead content paints as defined by British Standard No. 4310. They are suitable for preparing surfaces that may be chewed by young children. These primers give great durability and excellent adhesion, and they may be used with confidence on all types of hardwoods and softwoods, provided that they are not highly resinous (see 'Knotting', p. 37). These primers should be applied as a first coat on all new timbers and on older timbers that have been completely stripped for repainting. They may be purchased in either white or pink.

Aluminium sealer and wood primer. This is a primer that is especially suited and recommended for use on highly resinous woods (p. 66). It is specially advised when the painting of Columbian and Oregon Pine, Iroko, Makore, Gurjun, or Afrormosia is contemplated.

Combined acrylic primer/undercoats. This is a water-borne primer that dries quickly and performs the function of both primer and undercoat on hardwood and softwood alike. It is not necessary to use knotting on most woods unless there is exceptional resin content. It is particularly suitable for use on items made from man-made boards used in the construction of internal doors, cupboards and kitchen units.

Undercoats are applied after a primer has been used. They help to cover minor blemishes by virtue of their consistency and opaque nature. They afford excellent adhesion and provide a basic colour base for the final 'finishing' coats. They have great covering power and are oil-based.

Gloss finish (liquid) gives a high quality finish, internally or externally. It is hardwearing and weather-resistant. The more modern gloss paints from the better manufacturers are such that brushes, rollers and pads need only to be cleaned in water, preferably warm, to which a little household detergent has been added. There are, however, many types and brands that still need to be cleaned off applicators with turpentine or white spirit. Even these are better for a final wash in soap and water.

Gloss finish (non-drip) may also be used

for both internal and external use. It is drip-resistant and therefore of considerable interest to the amateur DIY decorator. It has rather less covering power per litre than liquid gloss, but brushes, rollers and pads may be conveniently cleaned in water, preferably warm, to which a little washing-up liquid has been added.

Gloss finish (vinyl) is only suitable for internal decorating. It is quick-drying and retains full natural coloration. It is emulsion based so that brushes, rollers and pads may be cleaned in running water.

Eggshell finish is an oil-based paint which gives a soft-sheen finish. It is suitable for internal use only.

Flat finish paint gives a non-gloss finish; it is used mainly in bedrooms, dining rooms and lounges where dirty conditions are not anticipated. Although light surface marks may be removed with a cloth and warm water, excessive pressure will lead to a breakdown of the surface. Some manufacturers market a specially pigmented version for painting ceilings to hide unevenness and staining.

Emulsion paints. There are three main types of these:

- Vinyl matt: an easy-to-clean, matt-textured, low sheen finish for walls and ceilings
- Vinyl silk: washable and giving a mid-silk sheen for use on walls and ceilings. It is especially suitable for coating relief wall coverings
- Mould-resistant external emulsion: for use on exterior walls subject to damp or mould build-up.

Brushes, rollers and pads used with these paints may be cleaned in water.

Aluminium paint is ideal for effectively 'killing' one distinct colour before applying another totally different one.

Paints for metal

All forms of ferrous metals are particularly susceptible to attack from rust, especially where damp conditions prevail. It is important, therefore, to protect the surface of these metals. Success here depends upon:

- The care and thoroughness with which the initial preparation is carried out. A rough and ready way is to use a wire brush, wire wool and emery cloth to remove existing rust. This method is seldom 100 per cent effective, and there exist proprietary preparations for treating the surface of metals. These preparations may be obtained from local hardware stores and body repair garages
- The type and quality of the primer used
- The thickness and evenness of the final 'finishing' coats.

Red lead metal primer is for use on iron and steel.

Chromate metal primer is a general-purpose metal primer for use on all ferrous metals, aluminium and aluminium alloys, galvanised iron and composite wood/metal structures.

Both of these primers are suitable for brushing on, white spirit being the medium for brush cleaning.

Special rust-preventative paints. There are a variety of these on the market, and if one of these proprietary brands is used, a primer is not normally required.

Iron oxide paint. If, for protective purposes, a maximum film thickness is required, one of these paints should be applied before the final gloss coats are brushed on.

Undercoats. See comments on undercoats for wood.

Gloss (liquid and non-drip). Eggshell, flat (internal use only) and aluminium—see comments on gloss paints for wood.

Paints for masonry, concrete, brickwork, etc.

If the painting of external masonry is contemplated, two potential causes of difficulty are dampness and the alkaline content of the surface to be coated. Particularly on new buildings, it is essential to allow for complete drying out to take place before attempting to paint. On older buildings the cause of the dampness must be tracked down and, where finances allow, eliminated if possible. You must choose the time of year that will allow the maximum opportunity for complete drying out. Where the alkaline content gives trouble (it will show as a white deposit on the surface), you must use one of the alkaline-resistant paints described below.

Standard primer sealer is for use on dry, friable surfaces and where there is high suction.

Alkaline-resistant primer must be used on all new brickwork, concrete and plaster or any other surface known to have an alkali content.

Masonry sealer is a special sealer designed to seal powdery surfaces. It also serves as an excellent undercoat for emulsion paints and the special mould-resistant paints.

Undercoats. See comments on undercoats for wood.

Gloss (liquid and non-drip). Eggshell, flat and emulsion paints. As for wood and metal (see above).

Cement-based paints resist dampness and seal surfaces well. The surface to be treated should be dampened before applying the paint. They are supplied in a rather limited range of colours.

All paints applied to masonry, concrete, brickwork, etc., are best applied by brush. It should be noted that all primers used on masonry work need adequate time to dry very thoroughly. Under adverse drying conditions, extra time should be allowed to ensure that thorough drying occurs.

Paints for building boards, sheets, slabs and papered surfaces

Standard primer sealer should be used on plaster board, papered surfaces, paper-faced boards and fibre-insulating boards, but not fire-resistant boards.

Alkali-resistant primer should be used on asbestos sheeting, all alkali-containing slabs of all types, and fire-retardant fibre-insulating boards.

Acrylic primer undercoat is a combined sealer and undercoat. It may be used on all types of board and is quick drying.

Finishing paints. See 'Gloss' for masonry, concrete, etc.

Paints for floors

Some concrete or composition floors are often painted, not only for the sake of appearance but in order to counter the 'dusting' effects of wear and to preserve the surface. Floors to be painted must be absolutely dry to eliminate the possibility of flaking and blistering of the paint. To this end, for lasting cure, such floors should be above the damp-proof course or, in very old properties, must be provided with total coverage by a waterproof membrane, such as polythene sheeting of 250 g thickness.

Floor paint. This is a special paint designed exclusively for use on floors. It may be applied by brush, roller or spray gun. In practice, it has been found that on most surfaces the roller is the quickest method, also giving the best surface finish. Two coats are required for normal floors, the first coat being thinned slightly, with ten parts of paint to one part of white spirit. On areas of exceptional wear, such as near doors and around intensive work areas, a third coat should be applied.

Paints for exceptional conditions

These must be used when painted surfaces may be required to resist the effects of chemicals, erosion of exceptional proportions, mechanical attack and where limitations are imposed in the form of time factors in drying.

Quick-drying primers and enamels are available for use where conditions make quick drying a necessity.

Alkali-resistant primers are to be used on asbestos sheets and fire-retardant sheets and boards where maximum resistance to fire is a high priority.

Chlorinated rubber paints (primer and finishing). There are a number of these on the market, designed to resist attacks by chemicals. They give a thick coating and must be applied by brush.

Special rust-preventative paints. See comments on paints for metal.

Having decided which paints are most suitable for your particular requirements in the existing physical conditions, you will need to decide on the colours and textures that you prefer. Most of the larger manufacturers provide a very wide range of colours and will provide you with free colour and texture charts. Many back this up with a technical advisory service. These ranges vary from time to time, some colours being added and some withdrawn. Never hesitate to avail yourself of the help that the advisory services offer. They readily provide guidance to assist you in making the most of your varying rooms with their differing needs.

You will need to purchase brushes and, possibly, a roller and tray or a set of pads. Let us look, then, at a range of these essential items of equipment.

Brushes

You have two clear choices—to buy top grade expensive brushes or lesser quality, cheap brushes. If you intend to use your brushes over and over again, then choose the best that you can afford and buy really good quality equipment. If your job is a 'one-off' effort, the cheaper alternative may suit your purpose. Which choice you make will depend on the scope of work you have in mind. It is, however, no use buying good quality brushes and then skimping the cleaning and maintenance of them—you will soon lose a lot of money that way.

Range of suitable paint brushes

Good brushes hold more paint than cheap ones because their bristles are 'flagged'; this is a form of tapered splitting at the ends. Genuine hog bristles are naturally 'flagged', but constant washing tends to soften them unduly. Hog bristles are now largely superseded by nylon bristles, which are 'flagged' during manufacture. Good quality bristles retain their spring and elasticity and maintain their shape under prolonged use and pressure.

When buying your brush, check it for loose bristles. If they exist when you are examining them, you may be assured that they will leave the brush in larger numbers as soon as you start to paint, thus causing a great deal of trouble and annoyance. Look closely at the base of the bristles to see if they are close-knit, with no gaps or pockets to hold paint. If such gaps exist, reject the brush, for it will be the cause of unexpected 'floods' of paint from time to time, giving rise to 'runs'. If you plan to do a great deal of painting at any one time, be sure that the handle is comfortable; badly designed handles can cause muscle fatigue and even cramp. You will need a change of brush from time to time if you plan to decorate a whole house, and reference back to Chapter 2 will give you the recommended range for this purpose. If you possess a house with Georgian-type window frames, you will need an additional brush, called an angled sash brush; this will make the painting of the small individual frames much easier.

Rollers

As with brushes, you have the choice of cheap or more expensive rollers. If you only intend to use your roller once, there is little point in purchasing an expensive one. If, on the other hand, you intend to cover a large area, and use your roller over and over again, then you will be well advised to go for the more expensive alternative. Assuming that you purchase the more expensive roller, you should ensure that the core is of 'cage-like' construction rather than a tube, as this will facilitate removal of the roller. Be careful

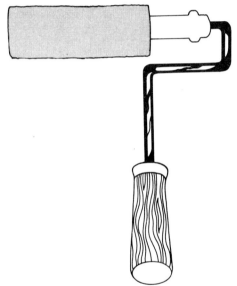

to choose a roller where the 'nap' or cover is formed over a plastic base so that it does not soften after repeated washings. The depth of the cover 'nap' is determined by the surface that you wish to paint, so you will be well advised to purchase two covers, one 6 mm ($\frac{1}{4}$ in.) deep for general purpose work and one 9 mm ($\frac{3}{8}$ in.) deep for the painting of rough surfaces, such as concrete or brickwork. Standard rollers are 150 mm (6 in.) wide, but you will need one 175 mm or 200 mm (7 in. or 8 in.) wide for large wall areas.

Selection of the proper 'nap' material is all-important for a really good finish.

There are three main types:

- **Nylon:** a synthetic material recommended for use with water emulsion-based paint, although it can be used successfully with oil-based paint.
- **Lambswool:** to be used with oil-based paint only, never with water-based emulsion paint; it will absorb water and be ruined.
- **Mohair:** a natural material with a 6 mm ($\frac{1}{4}$ in.) 'nap' that provides the smoothest possible finish when using gloss, semi-gloss, enamel, lacquer or varnish finishes. Cheaper rollers have a polyurethane foam applicator. They are suitable for general use. They are difficult to clean thoroughly but are cheap enough to throw away after use.

Special rollers

If you intend to paint ceilings, make sure that the handle of your roller is designed to take extension handles. Handy, small rollers, 25–75 mm (1–3 in.) wide, are available for painting 'trim' and window sashes and there are small, cone-shaped rollers for getting close into corners, but these require a little practice to use successfully.

Paint tray

This is an essential piece of equipment for use in conjunction with your roller. You should ensure that the tray you choose is equipped with a metal-mesh grid for removing excessive paint from the roller, thus avoiding unsightly 'runs' and 'curtaining'.

Pads

These are relative newcomers to the list of applicators. They are supplied in a range of sizes, the largest being about 150 mm × 100 mm (6 in. × 4 in.). The pad is covered by short bristles about 6 mm ($\frac{1}{4}$ in.) long and the range of materials for these 'naps' is similar to those for rollers. They are easy to use and cover large areas quickly. They are well worth trying; most amateurs find them easier to control accurately than rollers, and you may well find you can use them with greater precision when working right up into corners.

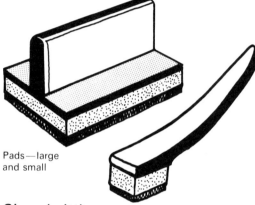

Pads—large and small

Glove (mitt)

These are lambskin-covered gloves that are worn on the hand. They are ideal for painting irregular surfaces such as pipes, grills, radiators.

Spray equipment

Although the brush, roller and pad are the most commonly used applicators in the home, a great deal of the hard work can be eliminated by using spray equipment. After a little practice, a high standard of work can be achieved with a great saving of time; a job normally taking, say, four hours can be done in one hour. It cuts out a great deal of physical work and a much more uniform spread can be achieved, with a considerable saving of paint. Practice makes perfect and, to ensure a good job, considerable experience is required. To buy a good set of spray equipment is very costly and you should try hiring the type of apparatus you require from a local hire firm. Your local paint dealer can advise you where to arrange the hire.

For the amateur home decorator, the pressure-feed spray gun is the most useful all-round type. With this form of gun you can use both internal mix and external mix nozzles. By ringing the changes you can, with these two, cover the whole range of house painting requirements. An internal nozzle mixes the paint and air inside the nozzle and this arrangement is best suited for the heavy-bodied paints. An external mix nozzle allows the paint and air to flow separately; they mix just outside the gun, a combination best suited to the use of quick drying enamels, lacquers, cellulose and water-based paints.

If you do decide to purchase your own equipment, make quite certain that the two pieces of apparatus are correctly matched for the CFM (Cubic Feet per Minute) ratings; these will be stamped or plated on both items. For very small painting jobs, particularly in difficult places, the small, handy aerosols are very useful but very expensive to use on larger work.

Estimating quantities required

Paints vary greatly in their spreading capacities and surfaces, too, vary considerably in the amount of paint required to cover a given area. The average 'spread' of any given paint is usually indicated on the tin and you can generally take it that these figures are calculated on the basis of a working surface of average porosity. Increased consumption can be anticipated if the surface to be treated is rough textured or of high porosity or suction. The figures given below are average ones for surfaces of average porosity.

When estimating how much paint you will need to buy, you will have to take into consideration all the above-mentioned factors, plus the number of coats you may deem it necessary to apply. Remember that you will need fewer coats if you are not radically changing the colour. When the existing paintwork is in good order you may get away with only one coat but, generally, you can reckon on two coats as an average requirement.

PAINT	AVERAGE SPREAD RATE PER 5 LITRES	
Primer (White or Red)	40 Sq. Metres	48 Sq. Yards
Aluminium Sealer	80 ,, ,,	95 ,, ,,
Acrylic Primer/Undercoat	55 ,, ,,	65 ,, ,,
Alkali Resistant Primer	35 ,, ,,	45 ,, ,,
Primer/Sealer	45 ,, ,,	55 ,, ,,
Masonry Sealer	60 ,, ,,	70 ,, ,,
Red Lead Metal Primer	40 ,, ,,	50 ,, ,,
Chromate Metal Primer	55 ,, ,,	65 ,, ,,
Undercoat	55 ,, ,,	65 ,, ,,
Gloss (Liquid)	85 ,, ,,	100 ,, ,,
Gloss (Non-Drip)	60 ,, ,,	70 ,, ,,
Eggshell Finish	80 ,, ,,	95 ,, ,,
Flat Finish	80 ,, ,,	95 ,, ,,
Emulsion (Matt) — These vary very widely because of thinning variations in use	70 ,, ,,	85 ,, ,,
Emulsion (Vinyl Silk)	75 ,, ,,	85 ,, ,,
Aluminium Paint	90 ,, ,,	105 ,, ,,
Mould and Damp Resistant Paint	35 ,, ,,	40 ,, ,,
Floor Paint	45 ,, ,,	50 ,, ,,
Polyurethane Varnish (Glossy or Satin)	90 ,, ,,	110 ,, ,,
Varnish (Exterior Quality)	90 ,, ,,	110 ,, ,,

Some colours, especially reds, yellows and greens, have a poorer covering power than whites, creams and duller colours and, in some cases, you may need three coats before a solid appearance is obtained.

Now to calculate the actual quantity of paint required. Rectangular areas such as plain walls and ceilings present no real problems. Measure length and width (height) so that:

Length × Width = Area in square metres

Ignore windows and doors so that you will have a little paint in hand. This is far better than running short at a crucial time, and it will provide you with a supply for 'touching-up' the odd scratch or knock that invariably occurs in any home.

Now divide 'A' (the Area) by the Spread Rate (SR) given in the table after reducing it to Spread Rate per litre. (Since the given figure refers to spread rate per five litres, the normal, economical size of can to buy, divide it by five.) This will then tell you how many litres *per coat* you will require for the job:

$$\frac{L \times W}{SR \text{ per litre}} = \frac{A}{SR \text{ per litre}} = \begin{matrix}\textbf{Number}\\ \textbf{of litres}\\ \textbf{per coat}\end{matrix}$$

For example: a room 5 metres long × 4 metres wide and $2\frac{1}{2}$ metres high would require the following amount of matt emulsion paint:

| 4 | 5 | 5 | 4 | $2\frac{1}{2}$ |

WALLS:

$$\text{AREA} = \frac{18 \times 2\frac{1}{2}}{14}$$ (Spread Rate of matt emulsion per litre)

$$= \frac{45}{14} = 3\frac{1}{4} \text{ litres (approx.)}$$

CEILINGS:

$$\text{AREA} = \frac{5 \times 4}{14} = \frac{20}{14} = 1\frac{1}{2} \text{ litres (approx.)}$$

So, for one coat, you would require $3\frac{1}{4} + 1\frac{1}{2} = 4\frac{3}{4}$ litres; so you would buy a 5 litre can. Most paints are sold in $\frac{1}{2}$, 1, $2\frac{1}{2}$ and 5 litre cans, it being cheaper to buy the larger sizes.

Woodwork and 'trim'

This includes doors, windows and skirting boards. In estimating the amount of paint required for these, it is common practice to take a standard door as the basic unit. These average out at 2 m × $\frac{3}{4}$ m ($6\frac{1}{2}$ ft. × $2\frac{1}{2}$ ft.). Allowing for the frames and door trims, etc., this works out at approximately 2 square metres per door.

Windows vary so much in shape and size that only a very general indication can be given and this is generally calculated on the following basis:

1 small window = 1 door (2 sq m)
1 average window = 2 doors (4 sq m)
1 large window = 3 doors (5 sq m)

Skirtings in modern houses are usually 75–125 mm (3–5 in.) wide. If we take an average room measuring 5 m × 4 m (approx. $16\frac{1}{2}$ ft. × 13 ft.), this would give 18 m of skirting board, giving a total area of approximately 2 sq m, = 1 'door unit'.

So, to calculate the amount of paint required to cover all woodwork and trim, you will need to know the total number of 'door units' (including windows and skirtings as above).

For example, in a typical bedroom with one door, one small window and one average window, and with 18 m of skirting, you would have the following 'door units':

Door . .   . . 1 unit (2 sq m)
1 small window . . 1 unit (2 sq m)
1 medium window   2 units (4 sq m)
Skirting . .   . . 1 unit (2 sq m)
Total = 5 units (10 sq m)

This, based on the spread rate for matt emulsion (see the table on p. 21) will require $\frac{3}{4}$ litre of paint.

External calculations

These are, basically, similar, but remember to allow about double the standard 'trim' allowance on windows and doors to cater for gutters, drainpipes, etc., if these are not of the modern plastic type. A general guide, for a typical semi-detached house, measuring 8 m × 7 m (26 ft. × 23 ft.) in plan, with an average wall height of 6 m (20 ft.), would be as follows:

Total wall surfaces
(smooth) .. .. 14 litres per coat
Total wall surfaces
(rough) .. .. 30 litres per coat
Woodwork and trim .. 3 litres per coat

These calculations are based on the average spread rate rather than that of one particular type of paint, since the variations are negligible when dealing with such a large quantity of paint.

Estimating time

This is a difficult one! People work at very different rates and no house is without its special problems. Below is given a chart, worked out on broad average lines, geared to the amateur decorator and based on an eight-hour working day, with a tea or coffee break every two hours or so. You will find that you need these 'breathers' and you will return to your work refreshed.

Square metres per hour

1. On smooth surfaces

Priming and sealing ..	10
Flat finish paints, including emulsions	9
Gloss or semi-gloss paint ..	10

Allow 20% less time for each subsequent coat

2. Doors, windows, skirtings, etc.

Sanding and filling ..	10
Priming/sealing	15
Painting (first coat) ..	8
Painting (each subsequent coat)	9
Enamelling	5
Varnishing	10
Staining (floor boards) ..	10

3. Ceilings

Priming and sealing ..	9
Flat finish paint	8
Gloss or semi-gloss paint ..	6

Allow 20% less time for each subsequent coat

4. Painting floors

First coat	14
Additional coats ..	16

5. Painting brickwork, concrete, pebble dash

First coat	6
Subsequent coats	7

Costs

No specific details are really possible, as costs will depend so much on current prices, which vary widely from month to month. There is little to choose between the leading manufacturers, but by shopping around you can find quite a number of cheaper brands that can be quite satisfactory, particularly if used on internal work. Often large stores give substantial discounts of up to 50 per cent on marked prices on lines that have been discontinued. If you can modify your requirements to take advantage of these offers, you can save a great deal of money. Additional savings can be made by choosing colours that 'cover' well, thereby reducing the number of coats required to give a 'solid' finish. If you are prepared to have the same colour in a number of rooms, you can again effect a saving by buying the larger, more economical 5 litre cans. Such uniformity also saves a good deal of operational time.

4 · Painting (ii)

Preparing the paint. Painting ceilings, walls and woodwork. Masking. Alternative methods of application: brush, roller and spray gun. Cleaning and care of equipment. Storing used paint.

Now that you have prepared your surfaces, selected your colours, chosen the type of paint that you require, provided yourself with the necessary equipment, purchased the correct quantities of primer, undercoat and finishing paint and made a rough estimate of the time that the job will take you, you are ready to start your decorating in earnest.

Internal painting is the job most commonly undertaken by the amateur as a first excursion into home decorating. With the exception of some staircases leading up from the hall, most heights are reasonable, work is not interrupted by poor weather and, usually, less arduous preparation is necessary. If you have followed the advice given in Chapters 1, 2 and 3, you should be well primed to start painting right away.

Preparing the paint

Stirring

Although the paint should not be prepared until the surfaces to be painted are completely ready, and any platform, etc., rigged up, we will deal with it first. With the exception of non-drip paint, which quite definitely *must not be stirred*, all paints require stirring before use. If this is not done the paint may well dry out patchy or streaky and, even with the highest quality paints, if they have been in store for a little while the heavier elements in the paint will sink to the bottom of the tin. These must be stirred back into the fluid if the correct consistency is to be achieved; a really thorough stirring is

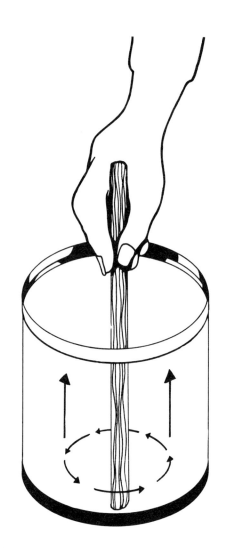

Stirring paint with a stick. Use a circular and up-and-down motion

necessary. Use a good substantial stick, about 300 mm–400 mm (12 in.–16 in.) long and about 25 mm–40 mm (1 in.–$1\frac{1}{2}$ in.) wide. Stir with a circular and up-and-down motion for at least five minutes or until the tip of the stick no longer brings up any solid matter.

Continue stirring until you have a completely consistent texture. If you bought your paint in the larger, more economical sizes ($2\frac{1}{2}$ or 5 litres), you should not attempt to paint from the tin but use a paint pot with a handle. These are now usually made of plastic material and can be bought for a few pence from any hardware store. Most are supplied with a simple brush holder that allows you to 'park' your brush safely while you are not actually painting; at the same time it allows the tip of the bristles to dip in the paint, thus keeping them flexible for immediate use again. These holders are also useful in that they keep paint from the handle of the brush. A piece of wire tied across the top of the tin can be useful for removing excess paint from the brush.

Ensuring colour regularity

If you have a great deal of painting to do and have bought several tins of one colour, you should remember that even with the best manufacturers, who exercise the greatest care in production, one batch may differ a little in shade from the next. To avoid patchiness or areas of different shading, you should 'box' all the cans. This means pouring the contents of all the tins into a large container and thoroughly mixing the contents together for several minutes, five at least, and then pouring the resulting mixture back into the individual tins. This may seem rather a nuisance but it really is worth the effort to ensure complete similarity of the whole painted area.

Removing paint skin

If you have reopened a tin of paint that has been used before, you may well find that a 'skin' has formed over the surface of the paint. If the skin is fairly thick, cut round the edges in contact with the walls of the tin with a screwdriver or old knife and then, with care, you can remove the complete circle of skin and put it on to an old newspaper. When this has been done, stir the paint thoroughly as described above. If, however, the skin is only very thin, you may not be able to remove it in one piece and you may well lose some of it back into the paint. Should this happen, or if for any reason the paint has lumps in it, it must be strained before use or a very poor surface finish will result.

Straining your paint

It is possible to buy paint strainers but it is really quite unnecessary for the amateur to do this since a discarded pair of fine mesh tights or stockings, without any holes in, are ideal for the job. Put the stocking over

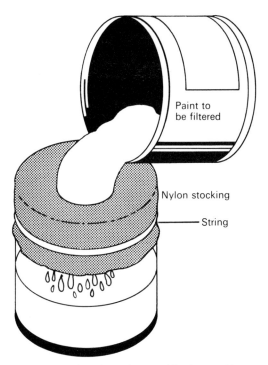

Paint to be filtered

Nylon stocking

String

How to strain paint, using an old nylon stocking

the top of a suitable container, not too tightly, and tie it in position (see p. 25). Now pour the paint slowly on to the home-made filter and allow it, *under its own weight*, to filter through into the container below. Do not attempt to push the paint through the stocking with any stick or spoon or brush or you will almost certainly push lumps through; you may even tear the nylon mesh and have to start all over again. This will, inevitably, take some time, so arrange to do some other little job while the straining is in progress, returning from time to time to add more paint to the filter until all of it has been treated. Be careful when you remove the stocking not to allow any of the filtered lumps to fall back into the paint.

Thinning

Most paints, other than water-based emulsions, are marketed ready for use, straight from the tin. Whatever you do, *do not try to thin non-drip paints* or they will lose the all-important non-drip pro-perty. If oil-based paints have to be thinned for any reason, say for use in a spray gun, or on porous plaster, some hardwoods or to restore the correct 'fluidity' of paint after it has been in use in an open container for some long time and is becoming 'tacky', then white spirit is the universal thinner, but do follow the makers' instructions to the letter.

To avoid excessive evaporation of paint while in use, pour out only a little at a time and put the lid firmly back on the tin from which it was taken. Most emulsion paints are ready for use but they may require to be thinned for use as 'sealer' coats or for application on very porous surfaces. Water is the general 'thinner' for emulsion paints, but add any water very sparingly and test after adding and before using. Remember, you can always add a little more water but the effects of over-dilution are not nearly so easily counteracted. Polyurethane and other special paints usually need special

'thinners'. In such cases, always follow the makers' directions, or you may well end up by ruining your paint.

Painting Ceilings

Always start with the ceiling, but if the floors are to be sanded (see pp. 37–8) carry out this job first to avoid any dust settling on freshly painted walls and ceiling. Be sure, however, to cover your freshly sanded floors with old sheets or discarded curtains to avoid spotting the floor with paint. Any furniture left in the room should also be completely covered. Sheet polythene is now available very cheaply and this provides an excellent waterproof cover at low cost.

Preparing to paint

If the ceiling is not greasy (for example in a bedroom), wipe it with a clean, dry rag or brush it with a soft brush covered with a duster. If grease is present, as is always possible in a kitchen, wash the area with a solution of trisodium phosphate, obtainable from your local chemist or hardware store, and then rinse over with clean water and allow to dry thoroughly before painting.

Remove all lighting fixtures or, where they cannot be removed, cover them over completely with paper fixed with masking tape. If you are going to use a hand brush or roller it will pay you to fix up a platform of builders' boards between two step ladders at a height convenient for you to work comfortably. A good guide is for your head to be approximately 150–225 mm (6–9 in.) from the ceiling. This arrangement will give you a wide working area, without frequent trips up and down your steps. Make sure that the boards are thick enough to take your weight without undue flexing and that the step ladders are well braced.

Now is the time to prepare your paint

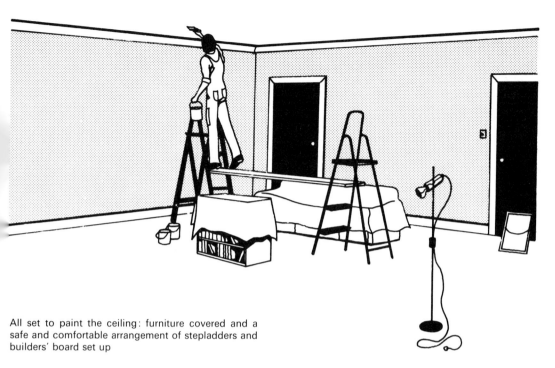

All set to paint the ceiling: furniture covered and a safe and comfortable arrangement of stepladders and builders' board set up

carefully; once that has been done, you are ready to get on with the job of applying it to the ceiling. .

Using a roller

If you intend to paint the ceiling with a roller, you will make the work easier if you use a brush to paint a border right round the edges of the ceiling about 50–75 mm wide (2–3 in.). This will enable you to use your roller on a long handle quite free and quickly. Border rollers are available or you can, as a further alternative, use a 75 mm (3 in.) pad.

When using a roller, do not hurry, but apply the paint slowly to avoid spattering it unnecessarily. It is best if you plan to do any work with a roller across the width of the ceiling, rather than the length. Start with, say, a 600 mm (2 ft.) strip at the edge of the ceiling, working into the border strip previously painted. Follow this 'to and fro' movement with criss-cross strokes to ensure complete coverage. After recharging the roller, make sure

that you begin in a dry area, working back into the area that you have just painted (see p. 28). Remember, always paint from dry to wet. By doing this, you will ensure freedom from join-marks and you will leave your work with a smooth, even finish.

However careful you are, you will find, upon close examination, little 'spatters' of paint in various places; for this reason it is advisable to wear an old hat when painting ceilings. Any such 'spatters' are best removed at once. It is easily done with a damp rag but, if left, the spats of paint will have to be scraped off, which can be a very tedious job.

Using a brush

If you decide to paint your ceiling with a brush, using emulsion paint, use the largest brush that you can comfortably wield and control. A 150 mm (6 in.) brush is ideal but, unless practised and experienced, you will probably find a 100 mm (4 in.) brush easier all round. You will find

When painting a ceiling, apply the paint in a criss-cross fashion

you will not need to change the brush nor start with a 75 mm (3 in.) strip all round the ceiling. You will find that you can, even with the larger brushes, paint right into the corners, but care is needed; above all, don't hurry. Once again, apply the paint in a to-and-fro manner, criss-crossing your strokes for complete coverage. Again, always work from a dry to a wet area.

Painting walls

This is similar in practically every way to the painting of your ceiling and needs little fresh description. It is obviously easier, since no special platform need be erected; nor are drips and spatterings likely to be so difficult to control. If a roller is used, however, a similar 75 mm (3 in.) margin needs to be painted around the top, bottom and side edges of the wall so that free, quick and uninterrupted use may be made of the roller. Remember always to apply your paint from a dry to a wet area.

that a 75 mm (3 in.) brush is quite big enough if you are going to use an oil-based paint but, here again, use a 100 mm one if you can manage it. Use the same general procedures as for a roller but, with care,

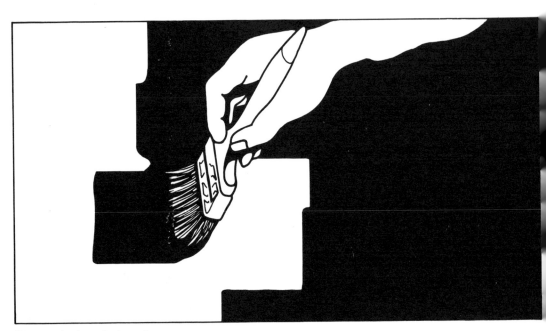

Always paint from dry to wet

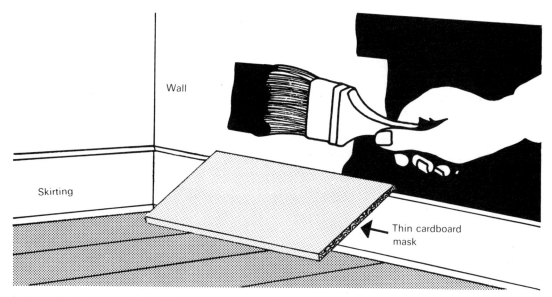

Wall

Skirting

Thin cardboard mask

Using cardboard as a mask to avoid getting paint on the skirting board when painting a wall or on the floor or carpet when painting the skirting

Masking

If the 'trim' (door frames, windows, skirtings) and floor are not to be painted, then some form of 'masking' will be necessary to avoid fresh paint getting on to them. One of the simplest and easiest ways of masking is to use a piece of thin cardboard, placed edgewise between the 'trim' and the wall, as shown above. Alternatively, you can use masking tape (see right). This is a thin tape, approximately 25 mm (1 in.) wide, which is self-adhesive, yet easily removed by lifting one corner and pulling. Masking tape applied to the edge of the 'trim' will allow you to paint right up to the edge. In many ways this is the better alternative, since there is always a risk with the cardboard mask, unless the greatest care is exercised, that in moving it along, some of the paint that inevitably gets on it will be transferred to unwanted areas. It may take some little while to apply the tape to the trim and may involve you in a small outlay but, once applied, it will enable you to apply your paint uninterruptedly right around the room in a free and flowing way. After

Window frame

Tape masking glass

Masking tape applied to the edges of window-panes will prevent paint getting on the glass when the window frames are painted

removing the tape, you may find a little paint has got on to the 'trim'; wipe it off immediately while it is still wet.

Removing fittings

You will find it easier in the long run to remove any electrical fittings or other items fastened to the wall before you start to paint. Removal of such obstructions will enable you to paint quickly and smoothly over the whole surface. Trying to 'cut in' around such fixtures is difficult and is a major source of annoying 'runs' of paint and if the fixtures themselves are not to be touched, they too will have to be masked off, which all takes time.

Painting over paper

If the room is wallpapered and you wish to paint over it, you must use latex paint, applied with a brush with nylon bristles. This will provide an excellent cover. Oil-based paint does not adhere to wallpaper and for this reason it should not be used. Should you, therefore, wish to paint a kitchen or bathroom and want to use an oil-based paint, you will have to strip off any wallpaper completely before painting.

When covering wallpaper with paint, examine the paper very carefully for any loose areas or bubbles. If these exist, apply fresh adhesive to the loose paper, having first peeled it back far enough to come up against an area that is firmly stuck. Cut through bubbles with a razor blade or sharp knife, expel the trapped air and restick. It is essential to provide a smooth, firmly stuck base.

Ventilation

Remember that when you are painting indoors, you must ensure adequate ventilation: open windows and ventilators. Some paints can cause headaches and nausea to some people, and a free flow of fresh air will help to eliminate these unpleasant symptoms and assist in drying out your paintwork.

Painting trim

'Trim' refers to doors, windows, skirting boards. When the ceiling and walls have been treated, you should next paint the skirting boards. Use your cardboard mask (shown on p. 29) to protect floors and freshly painted walls. If you have fitted carpets, these should be rolled back from the skirting boards or, better still, taken up completely.

Watch carefully the back of your cardboard mask; it may have become contaminated with paint after continued use and some of this paint may get on to your floors or walls. Any such paint should be removed immediately and completely with a clean rag. Apply your paint evenly, smoothly and sparingly. You will need a brush called a 'sash' or 'trim' brush 25–50 mm (1–2 in.) wide.

Above all, go slowly. This is a job demanding great care; it cannot be rushed if a good result is required. Doors should be painted in the order shown below.

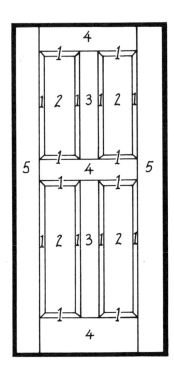

Use of a spray gun

Very few people use spray apparatus on a large scale in the home. It has, however, many advantages. It is very useful on large areas such as walls, particularly where there are only a few doors and windows to mask off. It is useful, too, on items of furniture such as cane chairs, open type screens and room dividers that would consume a great deal of time and care if brush-painted. If you do decide to invest in or hire spray apparatus, you will need to

(a) experiment with paint thicknesses
(b) practise before using with such things as distance from the surface to be painted, the movement of the gun across the area and the number of 'sweeps' to give good coverage
(c) find the correct nozzle size for your needs.

When you are ready to begin, follow these simple rules:

■ point the spray gun so that it is perpendicular to the surface to be painted
■ start spraying a little outside the area to be sprayed (to the right, left, top or bottom), to allow an even approach, thus avoiding unsightly 'runs'. Some masking may be necessary here
■ hold the gun so that you can achieve parallel sweeps along the surface. Do not swing the gun from the wrist, since this is a prime cause of uneven application
■ never stop in one place with the spray operative; this is another certain recipe for 'runs'
■ overlap your sweeps to obtain smooth and even coverage
■ always start with corners, rounded edges and mouldings first, progressing to the broader areas
■ remember that two or three fine coats are much better than one heavy application.

Cleaning and care of tools

Brushes, rollers, pads and spray equipment are not cheap items. On the assumption that you may be decorating your home for upwards of 30 years, it will certainly pay you to take great care of your equipment. Brushes, if well maintained, tend to improve with use over the years. Loose bristles are completely discarded and the tips of the brushes acquire a fine taper, which aids accurate application of paint.

Brushes, rollers and pads used with emulsion paint can be washed out in running water if cleaned immediately after use, but if the paint has started to harden it will be necessary to use warm water to which household detergent has been added. Should the emulsion paint have gone very hard on the brush, it may be softened by soaking in methylated spirits before washing as described above. After washing, the brushes should be dried out with clean absorbent paper or kitchen roll and the bristles manipulated back into their correct shape before being left to dry out completely. Ensure, however, that *all* the paint has been cleaned from the base of the bristles, since an accumulation of paint at this point will ruin the flexibility of the brush.

If pads or rollers have been used, the above methods apply equally, but do make sure that *all* the paint has been removed from the base of the nap. If oil-based paint has been used, brushes may be scraped clean of paint and then stood in a jam-jar of plain water if they are to be used again the next day or soon after. If they are to be stored for some while, they should be cleaned thoroughly in white spirit, washed in warm water with soap or detergent, dried off with absorbent paper from a kitchen roll and then left to dry out completely.

Some manufacturers are now marketing a gloss paint which only requires that the brushes be cleaned off in water to which detergent has been added, but always go by the makers' instructions. Rollers and paint pads must be thoroughly cleaned in white spirit, washed in warm water with soap or detergent and then dried off as for brushes.

Most people are quite tired after a long day of decorating and often just slip the brushes into a jam-jar of water, intending to clean them properly the next day. Unfortunately, these good intentions often get overlooked, the water in the jar evaporates and the brushes become hardened and are ruined. There are, on the market, several very good brush-cleaning liquids. If the hard brushes are immersed in one of the cleansers to the full length of the bristles, all they need, after 5 to 10 minutes' soaking, is a wash in warm water with soap or detergent. If they have gone very hard, they may be left in the cleanser overnight and then washed as above. The cleanser evaporates very slowly and, in extreme circumstances, you may leave your brushes soaking for days, or even weeks.

Brushes used with non-drip paint may be washed out in warm water with detergent, but this must be carried out immediately the brush has finished its job; delay, for even a comparatively short time, will find the paint hardening on the bristles.

When your brushes have been satisfactorily cleaned *and are quite dry*, they should be stored in plastic bags in a cool dry place. If your brushes are of natural bristles, you should add a little moth-killer to your bag, since they are vulnerable to attack by moths.

Spray equipment should be thoroughly and conscientiously cleaned. The gun should be cleaned by spraying solvent through it, after the container has been effectively cleaned, until no trace of colour emerges. This action should be carried out *immediately* after use. *Never use a pin, needle or nail* to clean the nozzle, as such treatment will almost certainly damage it.

You may use a bristle from a hair brush if the nozzle is not cleared by the solvent. Aerosol cans should be turned upside-down and operated. You will soon see a colourless liquid clear the jet, which will then be free and unobstructed for the next time that you wish to use it.

Storing used paint

When the job is over, either for the day or at the completion of the work, do not pour any paint left over in your paint pot back into the new tin of paint, for it will almost certainly be contaminated by little 'bits' picked up from the surfaces that have been painted. Rather, pour it into an airtight container (an old screw-top instant coffee jar is ideal) and label it. It can be used again, later, on some less important job or in some unseen place.

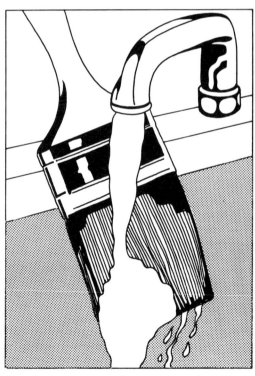

Most modern paints only require your brush to be washed out in water—sometimes with a little household detergent added

5 · Painting (iii)

Painting exteriors—use of scaffolding and ladders. Masonry and metal. Cabinets. Restoring and/or resurfacing floors: different types of stain.

Although interior painting is more popular with the amateur, the exterior painting of one's home is, physically, the more necessary and, hence, the more rewarding and money-saving. Interior decorating is mainly undertaken for aesthetic reasons, whereas external painting is essentially undertaken for the physical protection of the fabric of the building, in addition to the aesthetic appeal of a fresh coat of paint. The ravages of sun, rain, wind, frost and chemical erosion affect firstly the paint-work, and secondly the fabric and structure of the building. Neglect of exterior repairs and paintwork can rapidly bring expensive repairs in its wake. There is general agreement that the decoration of interiors should take place every five years and exteriors every three years. This is a reasonable 'rule of thumb' guide but, like all generalisations, it falls short of specific requirements. Some bedrooms, for example, can quite comfortably, with modern materials, be left longer than five years, whereas some exteriors, in exposed positions or in areas of heavy industrial pollution, need attention at least every two years.

Difficulties of painting exteriors

Some of the considerations that tend to deter the amateur from tackling exteriors with the confidence and enthusiasm with which he tackles interiors are: working at considerable heights, requiring the use of ladders and scaffolding; the limited periods during the year when this job can actually be undertaken, often coinciding with a limited holiday period or the pressing requirements of garden or allotment; and the far more arduous preparations that are usually required. These include surface repairs and preparations, the erection of scaffolding at some cash cost and, quite often, the replacement of rotted timbers.

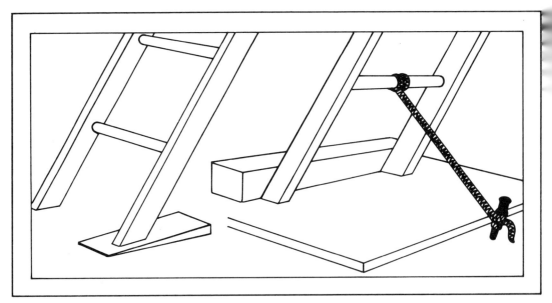

Ways of levelling and securing your ladder when working at heights externally. A softwood wedge measuring approximately 300 mm × 200 mm (12 in. × 8 in.) and tapering from 40–3 mm ($1\frac{1}{2}$–$\frac{1}{8}$ in.) will cover most needs for levelling purposes. A board measuring 450 mm × 375 mm × 18 mm (18 in. × 15 in. × $\frac{3}{4}$ in.), with a 50 mm × 50 mm (2 in. × 2 in.) block securely screwed about 25 mm (1 in.) in from the front edge, will provide a positive stop if placed under the end of the ladder, while a rope attached to the bottom rung and tied to a stout stake driven into the ground will give further security against slipping

Ladders

For most people it is virtually out of the question to buy scaffolding, and to hire it over the period that the average amateur takes to complete the job can be very costly. Because of this, it is essential that the DIY man or woman should acquire a lightweight, preferably aluminium, extending ladder, capable of reaching the highest point needed to be decorated, with at least 1 m (3 ft.) to spare. It still pays dividends, at the lower levels, to use a builders' board and two pairs of steps, even if one has to be borrowed from a friendly neighbour, so that greater mobility for long runs can be achieved—it is also easier on the feet and legs and far, far safer.

To leave both hands free, a wire hook (see right) can be bought or made (an old-fashioned meat hook is ideal) to hook over one of the ladder rungs and through the handle of the paint-pot. This can be moved up and down the rungs to suit your convenience.

A paint pot hook in use

Choosing the right time

Having prepared your surfaces, both masonry and wood, as described in Chapter 2, you will need to be critical in selecting the materials to be applied. You must plan your painting when the weather looks like being good for at least as long as it will take for you to apply one coat and for it to dry out.

The air temperature should, preferably, be above 10°C (50°F) with little or no wind. Do not start your painting until any early morning dew has dried off, and arrange to finish for the day in plenty of time for your paint to dry off (not necessarily harden) in the evening before dampness descends. For your walls, you will need the larger size brushes or rollers as described on pp. 18–9. Make sure that you have sufficient paint, boxed if necessary (see p. 25), to complete the job.

Paints for exteriors

Exterior paint is usually latex based. It spreads easily, dries quickly and uniformly, and there is now a wide range of colours. Alternatively, you may decide on a Portland Cement paint. This is specially useful in painting concrete or masonry that has not been painted before. It is bought in powder form and mixed with water in accordance with the manufacturers' instructions. There are some proprietary brands that are sold ready-mixed, but these work out considerably more expensive. These paints provide a very tough, weatherproof coating with an attractive texture at a very reasonable cost. Choice of colours is, however, rather more limited than with latex-based paints. The application of cement paints takes somewhat longer than latex paints. The surface to be painted must be thoroughly dampened before applying the paint. A large brush is to be preferred to a roller for the application of cement paints and the paint, once applied, must be kept damp for up to three days to give ample time for the cement content to 'set' rather than dry

out. Lightly spray it with water, using one of the cheap spray guns sold for use with garden insecticides.

A word of warning: should you, later, want to paint over a cement painted wall with any other type of paint, it will be necessary to use a special 'conditioning' coat first; consult your dealer about this. Walls that are damp, liable to 'dusting' or particularly porous should be painted with one of the special paints fully described in Chapter 3.

Procedure

Having decided which paint you are going to use, you should follow this procedure:

■ Decide whether a large brush or large roller will best suit your needs; you will need a brush, anyway, in order to reach those 'odd' places that elude a roller. Spray equipment is very quick, but can be more difficult for the amateur to manipulate, and the necessary masking can take up a good deal of time. Reread the paragraphs on spray-painting on p. 31 before coming to a final decision.

■ Start from the highest point that needs to be painted and work downwards.

■ At the highest levels, it may be time and labour-saving to do the 'trim' as you proceed, as this will avoid moving the ladder too frequently. You will, if you decide to do this, need your 'trim' brushes and paint-pot with you up the ladder.

■ Always secure your ladder carefully. Under difficult conditions of angle, tie a rung to some convenient point or, if the base of the ladder is on a lawn, tie the lowest rung to a stake driven into the ground.

■ Wear strong, thick-soled shoes; plimsolls are too thin and flexible for use on ladder rungs—they rapidly tire the feet.

■ *Always* keep one hand on the ladder. Use an 'S' shaped hook (shown and described on p. 34), to hold the paint-pot, leaving one free hand for the brush.

■ Use both hands, in turn, to manipulate the brush; this will enable you to paint a strip at least six feet wide before having to move the ladder. You will be surprised how rapidly you become ambidextrous! *Never* be tempted to stretch that little bit too far. It is far safer to get down and move the ladder — that way you will at least finish the job! If you have plants or shrubs below, cover them with old newspapers or an old sheet.

The number of coats you will need to apply will depend on:

■ the condition of the walls before starting
■ a possible radical change of colour
■ the porosity of the surface.

When the first coat is dry, you will have to be the judge. If the surface is uniformly covered and the colour is 'solid', then the one coat will be enough. It is, however, true that two coats usually give a much better finish, the second one going on much quicker and with far less physical effort.

Painting metal

Metals are quite the most difficult surfaces to paint satisfactorily and you will need to be very careful what you use in the way of paint. Study carefully the list of paint, their attributes and characteristics as outlined on p. 16, and prepare the surface to be treated. If it is badly eroded with rust, use a stiff, wire brush, followed by emery cloth and wire wool. A portable disc sander can be quite useful in this situation. When you have cleared the rust, wipe clean and wash with detergent, then apply a coat of rust-inhibiting paint before putting on your finishing coats, of which there should be at least two.

Metal rain gutters can be coated with a latex paint or zinc-chloride primer before they receive their top coats, or you may

prefer to use one of the bitumastic paints. It is essential to see that the surfaces are absolutely free from oil or any sort of grease. Items made from galvanised iron that has started to go rusty can be treated in this way.

On old aluminium surfaces, a powdery substance sometimes forms. This must be washed off with warm water and a detergent. The surface should then be painted with a latex primer before applying the required top coats.

Radiators and pipes

Before starting on the painting of radiators or pipes, you must make sure they are at a temperature no greater than room level. Neither must they be much colder, or water-carrying pipes may 'sweat'; so, you see, the temperature is rather critical. You cannot apply paint on very hot or wet pipes or radiators. On steel or iron fittings, you should apply a rust-inhibiting, red-lead paint before you apply your finishing coats. Copper pipes must have any of the blue-green deposit removed by very fine emery cloth or wire wool before being coated with a latex primer and subsequent top coats.

Kitchen and bathroom cabinets

Any type of cabinet, including refrigerators, can be made to look much fresher with a new coat of paint. Prepare the surfaces to be painted by washing with hot water and detergent. Then coat with a metal primer and apply several thin coats of good quality enamel. If you have one, or can borrow one, this is an ideal job for a spray gun.

Floors

Modern building techniques and the high cost of good quality timber have, between them, almost eliminated the true, wooden ground floor. What may appear, at first sight, to be a beautiful wood block floor may well be (and almost certainly will be in a post-war house of medium price) a concrete slab with 3 mm ($\frac{1}{8}$ in.) thick wood (or plastic, simulated wood) blocks, more accurately described as 'tiles'. You will experience very little trouble with such floors if they have been well laid. If poorly laid, you may be plagued with an epidemic of loose tiles. However, these may be readily and easily relaid using a black, bitumastic block adhesive, purchased from any large builders' merchant. If excessive wear occurs in areas of stress, e.g. in doorways and near French windows, the blocks may be removed and replaced by matching blocks. If it is impossible to match up the blocks, then blocks from unstressed and, if possible, unseen areas may be 'pirated' to obtain good blocks, replacing them with the thinner ones from the stress areas.

If you have a wooden floor downstairs, or one that needs treatment upstairs, proceed as follows.

Good surfaces

Examine the floor, devoid of furniture, lino, carpet or any other covering. If it is generally in good condition, you will need only to give it a good scrub over with hot water and a strong detergent such as trisodium phosphate. This will effectively remove all grease, accumulated layers of polish, and so on. If, with all this removed, you see no serious wear or protruding knots, all the floor will require is resurfacing with a good quality varnish. Polyurethane varnish gives a very hard finish and is virtually impervious to hot liquids that may be spilled on it.

Rough surfaces

You may, however, find that the hot water with which you washed the floor has raised the grain of the wood, leaving it with a rough surface. This will not be severe enough to require the services of a machine sander, unless you happen to have a small electric hand sander. All that you will really need will be a few sheets of medium glass-paper (grade F1) and a wooden block about 100 mm × 50 mm × 25 mm (4 in. × 2 in. × 1 in.). Wrap the glass-paper round the block and go over the whole floor *in the direction of the grain.* This will not take as long, nor be as arduous, as you might suppose, and it will result in a much smoother base for your varnish. When the varnish has dried, let it set hard before wax-polishing the floor. Use a beeswax-based polish rather than the cheaper, paraffin wax-based type; it will take a little more effort, but its wearing capacity and shine will be far greater.

Bad surfaces

Should you encounter several areas of considerable wear or sharply protruding knots, you will need to hire a large floor sander and a small floor sander. Additionally, it would help if you have, or can borrow, a portable, electric disc or orbital sander. If you are going to sand the surfaces of your floors, do so in the following sequence.

1. Remove all furniture, mats, etc.
2. Remove all curtains, pictures and, where possible, all wall fixtures and light fittings, because the sander does create a good deal of dust.
3. Close all doors but open all windows.
4. Prepare, and wear, a simple nose and mouth mask.
5. Use the large sander first with a coarse disc. It will tend, of its own volition, to move forward, so you will have to

A floor sander with bag attachment will obviate the worst of the flying dust arising from floor sanding

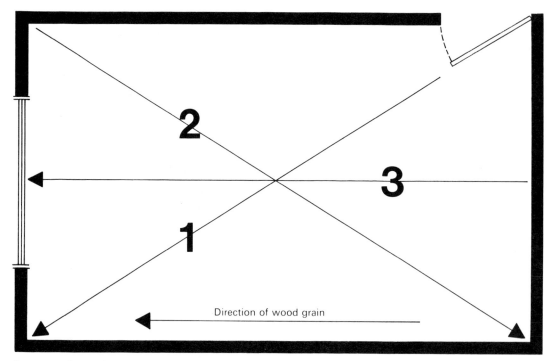

2

3

1

Direction of wood grain

Sequence of operations when sanding a wooden floor

exercise a slight restraining action to keep it under control. Proceed, as shown above, to work diagonally from one corner of the room to the opposite corner in a straight line. Once you have covered the whole room in this way, overlapping, slightly, each strip sanded, go over the room again between the other two corners. When you have done this, complete this phase of the sanding by going over the room again parallel to the longest walls or with the grain of the wood but, this time, using only a medium grade disc. Now carefully examine the surface. If it is not yet quite as smooth as you want it, go over it again, once or twice, finishing with a fine grade disc. Never let the sander stand still while rotating or it will sand a hollow in your floor that will be very difficult to remove. Inevitably, you will have some small areas still unsanded where it will not have been possible to

reach with the large sander, e.g. close up to corners, around fire-places, etc., and it is here that you will want to use the small, portable electric hand sander to complete your work.

6. After sanding, use a vacuum cleaner to remove all sand and wood-dust.

7. If you want your floor the natural colour of the wood, you can now give it at least two coats of clear varnish. The first coat will sink into the wood and almost disappear, leaving the wood a little darker but with precious little shine. The second coat will give a shine when applied after the first coat has been allowed to dry thoroughly. For perfection, you should lightly rub over the first coat with fine glass-paper (grade F1) before applying the second. For a really high sheen you will probably need a third coat, but if you decide to do this you will not need to rub down the second coat. After about a

week, the floor should be waxed with, preferably, a beeswax-based floor wax.

8. If you wish to change the colour of your floor but retain the natural appearance with the grain as a feature, you will have to use a wood dye on it before applying the varnish coats. These dyes come in three main types:
   - water stain
   - spirit stain
   - oil stain.

Water stain dye is purchased in powder form or in crystals. It comes in a variety of shades and is mixed with water, preferably warm. It should be applied copiously to the floor. It may well take up to twelve hours to dry and will certainly raise the grain to give a rough surface. To restore the surface for varnishing, it will have to be lightly rubbed down with fine glass-paper. *Do not press too hard,* or you may end up by removing some of the stain. Water stain is by far the cheapest of the three.

Spirit stain dye is probably the best of the alternatives. It penetrates the wood deeply, does not raise the grain, dries quickly and may be varnished or waxed. The better makes usually contain rot, fungus and insect inhibitors but they are by no means cheap. Spirit stains go on evenly but you will have to work quickly and evenly because of the fast-drying rate. Do not go over any areas twice, or you will have corresponding areas of dark colour. There are some proprietary brands of varnish stain on the market which do the combined jobs of dyeing the wood and producing a shine all in the one operation. They are effective but have two drawbacks:
- they are relatively expensive
- any subsequent coats materially darken the colour.

Oil stain dyes are particularly good for use on genuine hardwoods that are not required to have a very high shine. To this end, oil stained floors should be waxed and not varnished. Oil stain takes rather a long time to dry.

Painting a floor

It may be your plan to paint your floor in a colour of your choice. There are special deck paints which are excellent for the job, but the range of colours in this type of paint is limited. Alternatively, you could use a good quality Alkyd enamel which comes in a wider range of colours. For floors you will find that a roller is the best applicator, but a large brush is quite satisfactory. Always allow a good twelve hours between coats. You will find that, in all probability, you will need at least two coats, three on areas of stress. Paint tends to show wear rather quickly where the traffic is heavy but can be aesthetically pleasing. Painted surfaces can be waxed after a week or two, and this materially helps the wear problem.

Concrete, stone and composition floors may be painted as advised on p. 17. Not only does this present a pleasing appearance but it prevents 'dusting', which otherwise seems inevitable, especially on concrete floors.

6 · Wallpapering (i)

Selecting the most suitable covering: paper, vinyl, foil, textured papers, fabrics. How to estimate quantities and time. Preparing for papering; adhesives.

The term 'wallpaper' is now totally inadequate to describe present-day wall coverings. In any good local store, you now have a choice of the older wallpaper, vinyls, fabrics, woodchip, foil, burlap, cork, flocked and grasspaper coverings—all with their special physical features in addition to their various aesthetic appeals.

Coverings are now, in most cases, much stronger than previously, with greater resistance to tearing and surface damage. This makes them much easier for the amateur to hang successfully. A great many are washable and resistant to extremes of heat, while some are unaffected by steam and damp, making them ideal for use in kitchens and bathrooms. There are ranges that are marketed prepasted, so that all you have to do is soak them in water prior to hanging, and there is now a range which is applied directly to the wall after the wall surface has been pasted. This eliminates the job most amateurs dislike, namely the operation of carrying the wet paper from the pasting table to the wall, a process that so often leads to torn paper or damaged surfaces. With this type of covering, the pasting table is eliminated, together with the rather messy newspaper used to cover it.

Many coverings on the market are 'strippable', i.e. after lifting one corner of the covering, the whole strip may be pulled off the wall in one piece, thus eliminating one of the more tedious and time-consuming processes, that of stripping off old paper by means of soaking and scraping off with a scraping knife, which can be very messy. Earlier papers were sold to the customer with 'selvedge' edges, but all coverings now come ready trimmed. This, too, saves a great deal of time and helps with the hanging and matching.

Choosing your paper

Having decided that you are going to use a wall covering rather than paint in one or more rooms, how do you set about deciding which type to use? The following suggestions will help you to decide which type most suits your physical needs; you alone can decide on the pattern, texture, colour, and so on. The range today is quite vast; there are many reputable manufacturers, each with wide ranges in a variety of types. You could easily spend a whole day making your choice in the showrooms of some of the larger suppliers. Ask yourself these questions:

- Will the covering be used on walls in a high traffic area or one liable to be subjected to hard use, such as in a kitchen, bathroom, hallway or playroom for children?
- Is the room subject to a great deal of sunlight, calling for a fade-free type of covering?
- Does the room have difficult contours, such as the bedroom in a dormer house or one of the older types of house with odd-shaped rooms?
- Do you want a covering that is easy to hang in a comparatively short time?
- Are you set on a plain design or do you want a design that will have to be carefully matched at the joints, thus using more covering per wall?

Below are described some of the more popular types of coverings with their suggested applications.

Wallpapers

These are made from pulped wood and are suitable for bedrooms and other rooms not subject to extreme treatment or wear. They are produced in a very wide variety of designs. Some of the better ones can be lightly wiped over occasionally with a damp cloth. An adhesive is required for pasting the paper prior to hanging.

Washable papers

These may be easily washed with a damp cloth or sponge, using soapy water or detergent. Remove any grease, oil or fat at once, to avoid deep penetration of the paper. It is best if only a small area is cleaned at a time. Avoid wiping at right-angles across the paper, i.e. work up and down the strip.

Strippable papers

All that is needed to strip these papers is to lift one corner and pull the whole length of the strip away from the wall; no backing strip is left on the wall.

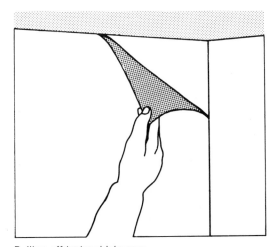
Pulling off 'strippable' paper

Vinyl wall coverings

Vinyl is a hard-wearing, tear and scuff-resistant covering. Vinyl coverings may be washed an infinite number of times without deterioration and are the ideal coverings for walls likely to be submitted to very hard wear and tear, such as in kitchens, bathrooms, hallways, playrooms and workrooms. Although washing will remove the vast majority of dirt and stains, very stubborn stains should be treated with methylated or white spirit first and then washed. A very wide range of colours and patterns is available. Vinyl has a very low moisture permeability, so that a special vinyl adhesive must be used for pasting vinyls in order to eliminate mould growth. It is essential that walls be absolutely bone dry before you hang any vinyl covering. All vinyl coverings may be stripped very easily by lifting one corner of the strip and pulling away from the wall. This will leave behind a base paper, which may conveniently be left to act as a 'liner' for any subsequent covering. Vinyls have a very high resistance to fade and should be used in all south-facing rooms.

Vinyl ready-pasted coverings

In most respects these are the same as the vinyl coverings described above, but they are coated with a special adhesive containing a fungicide. Upon the purchase of any reasonable amount of this type of covering you will receive, free of charge, a trough, usually made of plastic, in which to soak the covering before hanging.

Foil wall vinyl

This takes the form of a metallised film laminated to paper and printed with PVC inks. There is a rather limited pattern range. A good fungicide adhesive should be used with this form of covering. Butt joints only (see p. 50) should be used when hanging foil, and the covering should be smoothed down firmly, using a sponge or

41

soft brush to avoid scratching the foil. It may be cleaned by washing with warm water and soap or mild detergent. A word of warning—metallic foils conduct electricity and great care should be taken to see that they do not come into contact with bare wires, light switches or power sockets. For this reason, foil coverings should always be trimmed round switches and sockets and never be allowed to protrude into the casing of the light switch, etc. Foils tend to emphasise any imperfections in walls, so only surfaces that have been well finished and prepared are suitable to take this form of covering.

Flocked wall vinyl

This comprises a durable, self-coloured PVC film on a paper backing and printed with PVC inks. It is 'flocked' or textured with viscose rayon fibres, and provides an attractive, warm, soft surface. Flocked vinyls have a high resistance to wear and tear, abrasion and mechanical damage. A reasonable range of colours and designs is available. They are, quite understandably, more expensive than the more usual type of covering. They should never be hung on walls susceptible to damp, and a fungicidal adhesive should be used on them. Only butt joints should be used. They may be washed in warm, soapy water or mild detergent. They must be allowed to dry thoroughly and then lightly brushed to align the fibres of the flocking to even out shading caused by the criss-cross action used during washing.

Stubborn stains may be removed by using methylated or white spirit, followed by washing and brushing, as described above. They may be stripped in the same way as standard vinyls.

Wood chip covering

This usually has a thick, paper base speckled with fine wood grains (similar to sawdust) to give a highly textured appearance. Normally supplied in matt white, it is an ideal covering for ceilings that are uneven, or have poorly disguised joints or obvious cracks since, once in place, it tends to hide these faults to a very great extent, especially after it has been painted to the required colour in emulsion paint. Butt joints only should be used.

Fabric coverings

Hessians, velvets, silks and grass cloths are all used today as wall-coverings. Hanging them is really a job for the experienced professional and few amateurs will tackle them. However, wall canvas or dyed hessian can be quite attractive and, after you have had a little experience, you should be able to hang these. All have a paper backing and are supplied in standard sized rolls. A good quality, heavy duty adhesive is required. A 'natural' hessian can be purchased for painting to a required colour when in position.

Faced with such a choice, your decision of which covering to use can be quite a problem, but there are three main points which must form the basis of your final choice:

- the physical needs of the room

- the quality of your own skill and hence the ease of hanging in your home circumstances

- the price that best suits your pocket.

Calculating quantities

Once you have made your decision, you will want to calculate how much you will have to buy. Although there are some variants, most manufacturers have settled for a standard roll of pre-trimmed covering which is approximately 10.05 m long and 530 mm wide (33 ft. × 21 in.).

First measure your walls, including doors, windows, fireplaces, etc.; this will allow for wastage and awkward areas. As with paint, it is far better to have a little too much than to find yourself short at a crucial time. When you have measured (1) the total distance round the walls and (2) the height from the skirting board to the ceiling, use this chart:

Height in feet from skirting	Measurement in feet round walls including doors and windows													
	28	32	36	40	44	48	52	56	60	64	72	80	88	100
7 – 7½	4	4	5	5	6	6	7	7	8	8	9	10	11	12
7½ – 8	4	4	5	5	6	6	7	8	8	9	10	11	12	13
8 – 8½	4	5	5	6	6	7	7	8	8	9	10	11	13	14
8½ – 9	4	5	5	6	6	7	8	8	9	9	11	12	13	14
9 – 9½	4	5	6	6	7	7	8	9	9	10	11	12	13	15
9½ – 10	5	5	6	7	7	8	9	9	10	10	12	13	14	16
10 – 10½	5	5	6	7	8	8	9	10	10	11	12	14	15	17
10½ – 11	5	6	7	7	8	9	9	10	11	11	13	14	16	18

No. of rolls

Wallcoverings – how much do you need?

Height in metres from skirting	Measurement in metres round walls including doors and windows													
	9	10	11	12	13	14	15	17	18	19	20	22	24	26	30
2.00–2.20	4	4	5	5	5	6	6	6	7	7	8	9	9	10	12
2.20–2.40	4	4	5	5	6	6	6	7	7	8	9	9	10	11	13
2.40–2.60	4	5	5	6	6	7	7	7	8	8	9	10	11	12	14
2.60–2.80	5	5	6	6	7	7	7	8	9	9	10	11	12	13	15
2.80–3.00	5	5	6	6	7	8	8	9	9	10	11	12	13	14	16
3.00–3.20	5	6	6	7	7	8	9	9	10	10	11	13	13	14	17
3.20–3.40	6	6	7	7	8	9	9	10	10	11	12	13	14	15	18

No. of rolls

If you plan to paper your ceiling, the following simple chart will give you the number of rolls that you will require. All you will need to do is to use the measurement that you made for your wall quantities, i.e. the distance right round the room, including doors, windows, etc., and check it against the chart given below.

You will find that all reputable dealers have simple charts for calculating quantities and they are, usually, only too pleased to give you one and to help you with any queries that you may have in respect of quantities, quotations and suitability of materials for your particular needs. Do not hesitate to consult them.

Buying your wall covering

When you are contemplating the purchase of wall coverings, remember the following points:

■ Always err on the side of one roll too many rather than one roll too few. Manufacturers change their patterns fairly frequently and the one that you have chosen may be near the end of its run; you may not be able to obtain an additional roll should you find that you need one. All patterns are run off in batches, so you will need to ensure that all of your rolls are from the same batch. Should it be necessary for you to buy an additional roll and it comes from a

Paper for Ceilings

Distance round room in feet	No. of rolls	Distance round room in metres	No. of rolls
28	1	9	1
32	2	10	2
36	2	11	2
40	2	12	2
44	3	13	3
48	3	14	3
52	4	15	4
56	4	17	4
60	5	18	5
64	5	19	5
68	6	20	6
72	7	22	7
80	8	24	8
88	9	26	9
100	12	30	12

different batch, you could well find that the colour match, for example, is not perfect.

- Ensure that you have the correct adhesive (see below) for the covering that you intend to use.

- Remember that coverings with a predominantly vertical pattern or stripe in them will make a low ceiling seem higher and those with a horizontal stripe in them can, when applied to a narrow room, make it seem wider.

- Choose the paler shades for very large rooms, and avoid any blue in north-facing rooms (in the northern hemisphere) because the general effect will be far too cold. Avoid bright reds in bedrooms; they are too aggressive and unrestful.

- Practise on small rooms first—the bathroom, say, or a small bedroom, study or boxroom. Even if you do make a mistake here, the overall cost will be less and you will have gained very valuable experience.

- Buy the best quality covering that you can afford. It will hang more easily, largely eliminating the exasperating experience of paper splitting as you carry it or manipulate it into position on the wall. Thin, cheap papers split very easily when wet and they tend to stain badly if any of the adhesive gets on to the surface. The colours will run if you attempt to wipe off surplus adhesive.

- Always check the pattern and colours of your paper under daylight and artificial light. You will be surprised how some can alter in appearance under these differing conditions.

Preparations

Although wall coverings can cover surface imperfections much more effectively than any number of coats of paint, you will be well advised to prepare and repair your walls as outlined in Chapter 2, eliminating any causes of dampness at source, filling gaps and rubbing down with the same degree of thoroughness. Some imperfections still show through even the thickest wall coverings unless eliminated.

Have all your equipment, as described on pp. 12–14, ready and to hand, and remove as much furniture and as many fitments as conveniently possible. It is unlikely that papering will cause as much mess from 'spattering' as painting does, but a free floor and free walls speed the flow of your work.

Adhesives

You will need to prepare your adhesive, unless you plan to use ready-pasted coverings. Buy your paste where you buy your covering; your dealer will be able to advise you on the most suitable adhesive for the covering you have chosen. Vinyls, foils and fabrics require a stronger adhesive than pulp papers. Strengtheners can be purchased and added to paste if very heavy coverings are being used or if a particularly glossy surface is being covered, e.g. a gloss painted surface. Vinyls also need an adhesive with a fungicide added for complete protection against mould.

It is important to follow precisely the manufacturers' instructions for mixing. They will give a not too runny, not too thick consistency which will result in maximum adhesion. If you have mixed up a large quantity of adhesive, you may need to add extra water very sparingly after you have been using it for some considerable time, when it may tend to thicken up.

7 · Wallpapering (ii)

Where to start—using a plumb-bob. Cutting, pasting, lining up, trimming, rolling seams. Matching up patterned papers. Papering round corners and obstacles. How to paper ceilings. Using ready-pasted and wall pasted papers.

Where to start

Having selected your covering and purchased the appropriate adhesive, collect together all the necessary equipment and proceed to mark out the exact location of your first strip of paper. This is a most important part of your planning. If you are using a covering that does not require matching for pattern, arrange to hang your first strip to the right or left of a door or large window and then work towards the largest area of continuous wall surface.

If you have chosen a covering with a well-defined pattern that needs matching for motif, you should opt to start at a major centre of interest in the room, such as a fireplace. Arrange beforehand, however, that you do not end up with a narrow last strip in a prominent position. You may find that to avoid this, you will have to centre a seam on the starting point instead of centring the whole strip on the point. If you have a large, dominant pattern, you will have to decide where you want the pattern to start—will it look best if it starts at the ceiling line or if the ceiling line cuts the pattern in half?

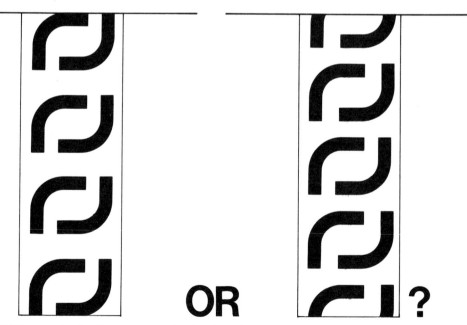

If your paper has a prominent pattern, you must decide where the pattern will look best in relation to the ceiling line

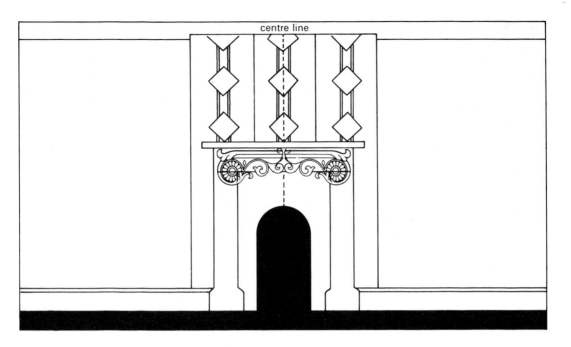

To give a balanced effect when hanging patterned wallcoverings, it is best to start from a centre point, such as a fireplace. There are two ways to do this. You can start your hanging with a strip in the geometrical centre of the chimney breast, or you can hang your strips on either side of a centre line. If you choose a 'drop' pattern, you would do best to use the centre line method since by so doing you will balance your large pattern units equally on either side of the chimney breast

Plumbing the wall

Once you have decided where you are hanging your first strip, you must then take what is, perhaps, the most important step in the whole hanging process. You need to 'plumb' the wall to ensure that you start off with a strip that is hanging perfectly vertically, failure to do this may well result in a papering job that gives the whole room a crooked or leaning look and jointing becomes a nightmare. Take your plumb-bob and line and chalk the line thoroughly. Pin the free end of the line to the ceiling at the level where the free end of the strip will be (see below) and allow the 'bob' to settle freely. Then hold it tightly, without letting it move, and snap the chalk line against the wall. This will give you a truly vertical line against which to hang your first strip. You are now ready to start your hanging.

Cutting and pasting

First cut your paper into lengths about 75 mm (3 in.) longer than the height from the skirting board to the ceiling. If you are using patterned paper which will require matching up, see p. 54 because it is not quite so straightforward. Make sure that you have mixed your adhesive according to the instructions, taking care to remove all lumpiness. A wire whisk, as used in cookery, is a useful tool for this purpose. Cover your pasting table with old newspapers, which should be quite dry. The ink on new newspapers is often wet and could come off on the face of the wallpaper. Be sure to paste the back of the strip very liberally and evenly, applying the adhesive with your large brush, pasting outwards from the centre of the strip as shown below. Do be sure that all the edges are thoroughly pasted; amateurs

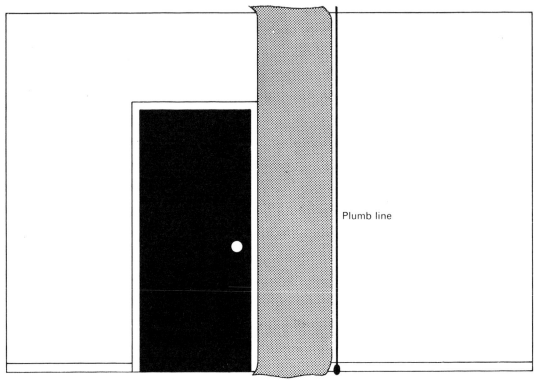

Plumb line

Once you have decided on your starting point you must plumb your wall to ensure that the 'free edge' of your first strip is absolutely perpendicular—irrespective of the door frame or corner from which your start is made

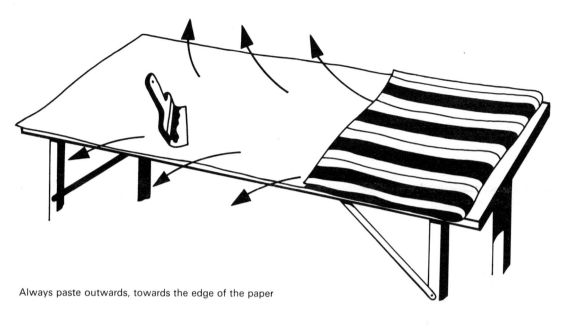

Always paste outwards, towards the edge of the paper

often neglect to coat these adequately and completely.

To take the 'curl' out of your rolls, particularly pulp papers, re-roll them once or twice in the opposite direction.

Folding the paper

To avoid drying out of the strip and to make it easier to carry when pasted, paste the top third of the strip and fold it over,

How to fold pasted paper to carry it to the wall

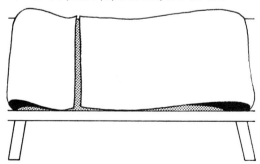

pasted surface to pasted surface, *but do not make a hard crease* at the fold. Then paste the bottom two-thirds and again fold the paper on to itself so that paste is to paste. Thus you will have only dry surfaces facing outwards, so that transporting the paper to the wall will be a clean, paste-free operation.

To allow the paste to sink into the covering uniformly and thoroughly, it is best to get on and paste a second strip before applying the first to the wall, i.e. always have one strip pasted while pasting a second. Before going on to paste a second strip, remove any newspaper that has become contaminated with paste and replace, so that you are always pasting on a clean, dry surface. Always have a clean, damp piece of rag handy for wiping off any paste that is on your hands or, in spite of all your care, any that has managed to get on to the surface of the covering.

Hanging the first strip

Remember that your very first strip is the really important one; get that correctly hung and the remainder follow comparatively easily. So make absolutely sure that strip number one lines up accurately with your plumbed line. Stand on your steps and unfold the top third of your strip, holding it carefully by the corners, but not too close to the edges or they may break away under the weight of the wet, paste-laden paper. Leave about 40 mm (1½ in.) of paper to overlap the ceiling for later trimming. Now carefully line up the top third of your paper with the plumbed line; lightly brush it on to the wall with your smoothing brush (see illustration on p. 51). Always brush outwards to the edges of the strip to ensure that you have removed any trapped air.

Any adjustment necessary for lining-up must be made at once, using the full palm of the hand to effect the necessary sliding movement of the paper. Now unfold the remaining two-thirds of the strip and gently brush on to the wall with your smoothing brush as before, taking great care to maintain the accurate line-up of the edge of the strip with the plumbed line. If, for any reason, it does not line up to your complete satisfaction, get a grip on the bottom two corners and gently pull away from the wall and reapply. Complete the smoothing process with the smoothing brush until the covering is flat against the wall and free from all air bubbles. If a stubborn bubble refuses to be dispersed, prick it with a pin to release the air and firmly brush down flat.

Joints and corners

If you are using plain paper that doesn't require matching up; the second and subsequent strips are applied and treated in the same way, sliding the latest strip to a tight butt joint (edge to edge, no overlapping), with the previous one. For patterned papers, see p. 54. Make sure that the butt joint is a tight one, since some papers have a tendency to shrink slightly when thoroughly dry.

When you come to the corner of the room, allow the strip to curve round for at least 25 mm (1 in.) on to the next wall. Even in modern houses very few walls are so true that room corners are absolutely vertical, and older houses can be very troublesome indeed in this respect. Butt jointing is almost impossible to achieve accurately, so one strip of paper will have to 'lap' over the other. Make sure that the roll of paper nearer the main source of light is undermost; that way, no hard shadow will show at the join. You must then rub this 'lap' down very well with a small joint roller (see p. 51). It may be necessary to use the plumb-bob again, on the new wall, to establish the true vertical.

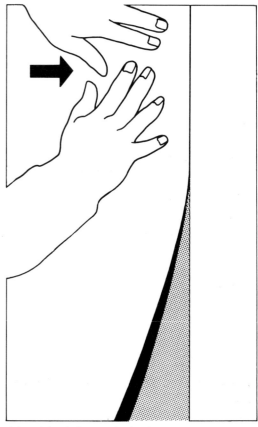

A butt joint (edge to edge)

Trimming

If you have cut your strips as suggested, you will have some overhang at both the ceiling and the skirting board. To trim these off, press the paper firmly into the corner made by the ceiling and the wall with your fingers or with a thick wooden rule, so that you make a clear, definite crease. You can now trim off the surplus in one of two ways:

1. Cut into the crease with a sharp knife, such as a Stanley knife, that utilises a fine blade similar to a razor blade. Razor blades can, in fact, be used but they can be rather dangerous and they can bend and cause inaccurate trimming.

2. After creasing, as above, pull the covering away from the wall, cut carefully along the crease with your shears and brush back into position.

Do not attempt to use a blunt knife on wallpaper; it will almost certainly tear it. Unless your knife is very sharp indeed, you must allow the paper to dry first and then trim. Repeat the trimming process at the skirting end by using either of the two methods described above.

Rolling seams

When the paper is nearly dry, roll up and down the seals with your joint roller (see below). If paste oozes out as you roll, then the paper is not yet dry enough; leave it a little longer before having another go. Rolling of the seams reinforces the complete adhesion of the paper at the joints, which is where trouble starts if adhesion is incomplete.

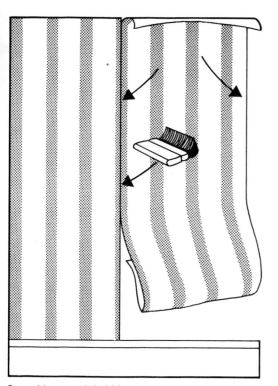

Smoothing out air bubbles

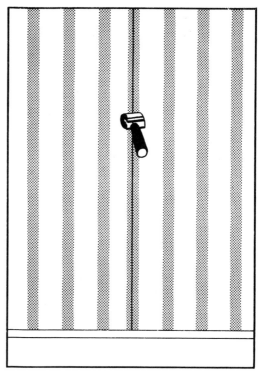

Using a joint roller to ensure neat seams

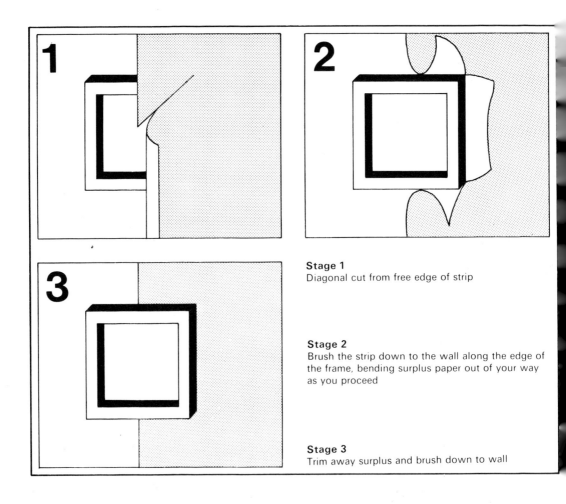

Stage 1
Diagonal cut from free edge of strip

Stage 2
Brush the strip down to the wall along the edge of the frame, bending surplus paper out of your way as you proceed

Stage 3
Trim away surplus and brush down to wall

Trimming round obstacles

Door frames and window frames are seldom difficult to trim to. Start by applying your strip to the wall in the way described above. When you come up against the corner of the frame, make a diagonal cut from the free edge of the strip in the direction of the frame, as shown below. You can now finish brushing the strip down to the wall along the edge of the frame, bending the surplus paper out of your way as you proceed. Treat all corners in this way and then trim away the surplus paper by one of the methods described above.

Wall plugs and switches can be treated in two ways:

1. Remove the surface covers completely after turning off the power at the mains. Apply your paper over the switch or socket and press to allow the switch button to pierce the paper. Cut a sufficiently large hole in the paper to allow the switch to function satisfactorily and reapply the cover plate to the switch. This method requires no accurate cutting or trimming round the switch plate but great care must be taken when using foil covering to see that it does not touch any bare wire, since it is a conductor of electricity.

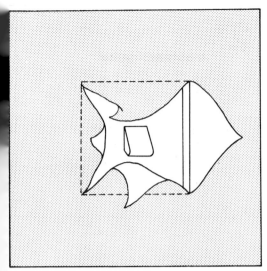

Trimming paper round a switch plate

Papering recesses

Recesses are fairly common in older-type houses and may present some problems for the amateur paperhanger. You will almost certainly find that the corners of the recesses are out of the vertical so that butt joints are out of the question. No two recesses are alike, whether they frame a door or house a cupboard on either side of a chimney breast, as was common practice some years ago, but the following procedures are common to most situations.

If you are using a wall covering that does not require matching, you will find the easiest way round the problem is to paper the recess first, cutting your strips of paper to suit the surfaces to be covered. When hanging the strips, lap the edges round each corner by no more than 12 mm ($\frac{1}{2}$ in.) or, if the walls are badly out of the vertical, by sufficient to allow for the 'out-of-plumb' dimension, making sure that you lap the strips so that the joint faces away from the main source of light.

2. Push the paper on to the switch button. At this point cut an 'X' in the paper and peel back along the creased edges around the plate. Trim in the manner described above. See above.

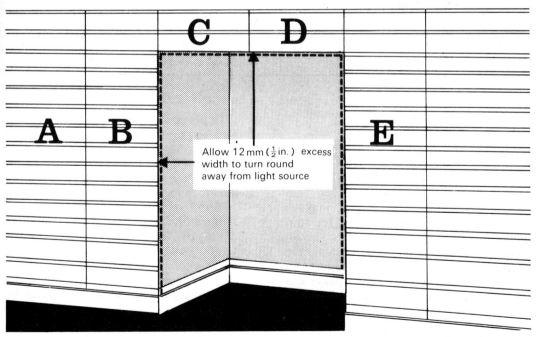

Allow 12 mm ($\frac{1}{2}$ in.) excess width to turn round away from light source

Procedure for papering a recess

Rub the joint down firmly with your roller when the adhesive is almost dry.

With your recess papered, proceed to paper round your walls as described. When you arrive at the vertical edge of the recess, cut your strip (B above), so that it overlaps the edge by 12 mm ($\frac{1}{2}$ in.), fold round so that the joint is away from direct view and roll down well with your roller. Strips C and D, plus any others that may be necessary to bridge the recess, should now be fitted and cut 12 mm ($\frac{1}{2}$ in.) too long, so that the bottom edge overlaps the top edge of the recess. Now paste and hang these strips and turn the excess under, rolling it down firmly. Strip E can now be hung with a 12 mm ($\frac{1}{2}$ in.) excess down the left-hand side. This excess should be turned round the vertical edge of the recess and firmly rolled down.

Should you have chosen a matching paper, you would have to hang the matched strips around the room first, ignoring the recess, but leaving 12 mm ($\frac{1}{4}$ in.) excess along the right-hand edge of strip D, the left-hand edge of strip E and the bottom edges of strips C, D plus any others necessary to bridge the recess; do not turn these excess strips round yet. Now match up the strips necessary to cover the recess and hang. When this has been done, paste the 12 mm ($\frac{1}{2}$ in.) excess on strips B, C, D and E, turn them under and roll down.

Matching papers

So far we have dealt only with the process of pasting, hanging, brushing-out and trimming with plain paper or with designs that require no matching. Should you choose a covering with a well-defined pattern, you will have to match each adjacent strip to ensure the accurate registering and continuity of pattern right round the walls. You cannot, for example, have half a rose at one point, a quarter of a rose at another, three-quarters somewhere else, and so on. Matching must be done

before you apply the adhesive and you will need to cut off at least two strips before hanging them. There are two ways of cutting off matching strips:
- Cut *all* your strips first, moving them up or down to achieve a perfect match, with the minimum wastage of paper, on all consecutive strips. Remember to cut off excessive waste at top and bottom to leave the recommended 75 mm (3 in.) excess for final trimming.
- Cut the first two strips only and match them, paste them and hang them. This enables you to check your matching each time and, for most people, this method is preferable, particularly if your room has a large number of openings or 'tricky' fittings or fixtures.

There are two types of pattern 'matchings':

Set patterns: these designs follow round the room horizontally.

Drop patterns: these match in a diagonal, 'downhill' direction. They tend to avoid a mechanical and, possibly, monotonous appearance.

You may find that to avoid undue waste, particularly on very large patterns, it is more economical to work from two rolls, cutting first from one and matching it with a strip from the other. Once you have matched the first two strips, all should then go smoothly. Remember, however, always to have one strip unpasted so that it can be checked easily for matching with the following strip.

Papering ceilings

This is a more difficult job than the papering of walls for four main reasons:
- Strips are invariably longer, and hence heavier, and more difficult to manipulate.
- Gravity works against you instead of with you.
- You will need some form of simple scaffolding.

■ It is difficult for the amateur to work on his own. You will do much better with a helper: he can 'hold-up' while you apply.

If you do decide to go ahead and paper your ceiling, there is no reason why you should not succeed, provided you adhere to two simple rules:

1. Paper your ceiling *before* you paper or paint your walls.
2. Paper the *width* of your ceiling, not the length, so that you have only to handle the shortest possible strips.

Preparation

Using a straight-edge and a roll of paper, mark off a straight line on the ceiling parallel to the wall from which you intend to start and the width of the strip away from it. This must be done very accurately and a helper makes this a great deal easier. Next, cut off your strips, checking carefully that you have measured the maximum width of your room: check this in one or two places since most rooms are not truly square. If matching is required, carry this out as previously described, remembering that you cannot match papers continually up one wall, across the ceiling and down the other side, since the design would finish up upside-down on the opposite wall. Allow, as with walls, about 75 mm (3 in.) extra on the maximum length for final trimming.

Arrange to have two pairs of steps and a long, thick, wide board so that you can apply the whole strip to the ceiling without having to get down to move the steps. Paste your first strip, as described already, but, because of its length, you will have to fold it ribbon-fashion (see above right) so that you can carry it and handle it on your scaffolding.

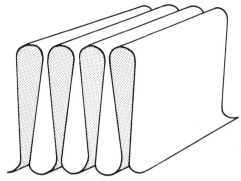

How to fold paper when papering a ceiling

Hanging the paper

Apply your pasted strip to the ceiling and allow 40 mm (1½ in.) overlap at the ends for trimming. If you have a helper, he should hold the strip while you apply the paper progressively, smoothing it out as you proceed and checking carefully that you are accurately lining it up with the pencil line that you have drawn parallel to the wall. If you are doing the job on your own, which is not advised, you will have to arrange to have a second board across the top of your steps to support the folded paper strips. This is a tedious process and many people will find working with their heads back and their arms above their head rapidly causes fatigue, possibly headaches and, in some cases, actual nausea; so, arrange to have several breaks while completing this section of your decorating.

Once the first strip is up, crease and trim off the waste at the ends as described above, before proceeding with the second and subsequent strips. Butt the edges as tightly as you can to ensure a good, smooth joint right across the ceiling, and roll the seams when the paste is almost dry. If your ceiling paper is white, plain, patterned or wood-chipped, you may want to give it one or two coats of emulsion paint; this helps to hide the joints. You will find, however, that on new paper at least two coats will be necessary.

Ready-pasted coverings

Wallpapers and a wide variety of vinyl coverings can be purchased ready-pasted. They are manufactured with a dry adhesive on the back of the roll. This adhesive is activated by soaking in water, for which purpose a trough is supplied with paper purchased in room quantities. When using ready-pasted coverings you will need to cut your lengths in the usual way and then roll each one up *with the pattern side outwards*. It should then be placed in the trough, which should be about three-quarters full of water. One or two minutes is all the immersion time that is required. The paper should then be withdrawn by the free end and applied immediately to the wall (see illustration). Some heavy coverings are best if additionally pasted, using thin adhesive applied liberally—this is particularly helpful if you are using exceptionally long strips, as in the case of papering staircases (to be discussed in Chapter 8).

When using vinyls, a sponge is preferable for 'smoothing-out'.

Wall pasted papers

A more recent development by some of the larger manufacturers is the poly-ethylene covering. This is not a paper, nor is it a vinyl. You do not need a pasting table and you paste the wall, not the covering. This is particularly helpful when covering difficult and complex-shaped walls, since the paper can be cut out dry to the wall

Ready-pasted paper simply has to be soaked in a water trough and lifted out

shape and simply applied direct to the pasted wall. It facilitates mobility since the paper is dry and, therefore, is in no danger of tearing in transit to the wall; again this is especially convenient when handling very long lengths for ceilings and staircases. As yet, the ranges are not so varied as in the case of vinyls. Stripping is easy; just lift one corner and pull away from the wall.

8 · Wallpapering (iii)

Coping with difficult rooms, awkward walls, and features giving rise to special problems. Staircases and new walls.

Sloping walls and ceilings

So far we have considered only the papering of reasonably straightforward vertical walls and flat ceilings. For many, however, it may be necessary to paper dormer bedrooms or loft rooms with sloping walls and ceilings.

Sloping walls and ceilings always present the problem of 'which is wall and which is ceiling'. If the slope is near to the ceiling, you will probably decide to paint or cover it in the same way. If, however, the slope ends, say, a metre from the floor, you may decide to treat it as part of the wall. A third alternative is where the whole wall slopes at one point, and in these circumstances it is usually best if it is painted or covered all in one way, thus presenting no real problem.

With so many variant angles and slopes, joining edges and matching can present considerable problems and the amateur is advised, if he chooses to paper the area, to opt for a plain or small patterned design that requires no matching. You should avoid papers with a clearly defined, vertical stripe in attics, dormers and loft rooms, since corners are almost certain to provide problems of parallelism of adjacent surfaces; they can look quite disastrous!

You may find, too, that butt jointing is difficult to achieve successfully, and you may be well advised to 'lap' your joints a little, going over them thoroughly with a joint roller afterwards (p. 51). The combined effect of the sloping surface and your paper will render these lapped joints virtually unnoticeable.

Pipes

In older buildings, and even in some modern kitchens and bathrooms, bare pipes may be found going round or up and down the surface of the walls. You will be well advised to try to use a whole strip and juggle it behind the pipes, rather than to try for a butt joint or a lapped joint directly behind the pipes. A helper can do a great deal towards making these particularly difficult operations less frustrating.

Awkward attic rooms can present special problems

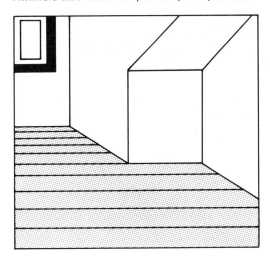

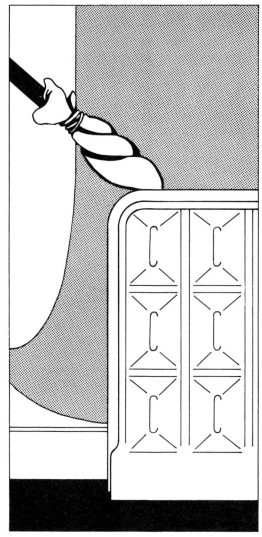

Smoothing down joints behind objects such as radiators can be greatly eased by the use of improvised equipment such as a cloth tied round a broom handle

Radiators

Do not try to paper behind radiators while they are hot; turn them off and let them cool down before attempting this rather tricky operation. With normal radiators the size they are, it is odds-on that you will have to butt at least one seam behind them. If you have started off as described in Chapters 6 and 7, you should not find this too much of a problem. If you can't get at the joint with your hand, try using a small paint roller with an extended handle. If there is not room to use a paint roller, get a broom handle and wrap and tie several layers of clean rag round it. You will find this improvised equipment quite helpful in smoothing out the paper behind the radiator (see left).

Friezes

Particularly in older houses, you may have to deal with a frieze, sometimes called a 'drop-ceiling', between the picture rail and the ceiling. It is customary to treat this as part of the ceiling rather than the wall and it should, therefore, be decorated in a similar way to the ceiling. If you decide to use paper, then you must apply your strips horizontally round the frieze to avoid multitudinous joints and short strips, leaving the customary trimming allowance at the ceiling and picture rail. As a frieze is usually less in depth than the width of a standard roll, it will probably be necessary to cut the required strip carefully along the length of the roll.

Poor surfaces—lining

If your walls or ceilings are badly crazed, cracked or of uneven surface texture, it will be desirable to use a lining paper before applying the chosen covering. In all cases the lining paper must be hung or applied at right-angles to the direction of the final covering. In the case of walls, the lining paper must be applied horizontally round the room so that the joints run across the joints of the wall covering. This is to avoid the possibility of coincidence between the joints of the wall covering and the lining. If you are lining the ceiling, then you must apply the lining lengthwise of the room before applying the final covering across the room. Under no circumstances must the joints of lining papers be lapped, or they will most certainly show under the final covering.

Staircases

To the amateur, decorating the staircase presents a real problem. While accessibility varies from house to house, there are always the common problems of the long wall running up the side of the stairs and the area directly above the stairs. Not only are these areas difficult to get at, but the length of the strips required makes them awkward to manipulate and hang. Moreover, you have to take into account the gradient of the stairs themselves.

The inaccessibility, coupled with the considerable height at which the operator must work, poses a safety risk, and nothing must be left to chance. The diagram below shows the safest and most convenient arrangement for getting at the walls with the equipment most likely to be found in the average home. By using a ladder, two pairs of steps and a strong builders' board as shown, it is possible to get an infinite variety of heights and positions that will enable you to gain access to the most difficult areas in safety. The ladder should, preferably, be of the extension type.

An example of a safe arrangement of ladders, steps, builders' boards and a box to enable the decorator to get at difficult areas when papering a staircase

Start papering with the longest length after plumbing a line one roll width from the angle of the wall (see opposite). You will quite definitely require assistance for this part of the job. Remember to allow an extra 75 mm (3 in.) for trimming as customary. Go on to cut all remaining lengths, remembering that, owing to the gradient of the steps, the short side of the first length is the long side of the second length, and so on (see below). As paper is expensive, and there are an infinite number of possibilities for error, it is safer, if a little slower, to cut one length at a time.

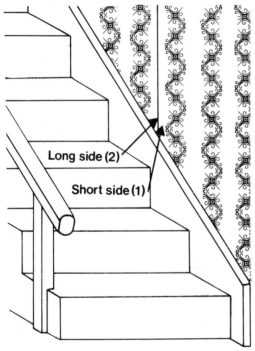

Remember—the short side of the first length is the long side of the second length, and so on

Paste your covering as described on pp. 48–9 and, if the first strip is less than 3.5 m (11½ ft.) long, make two folds. If it is greater than 3.5 m long, fold it ribbon-fashion as described for ceiling papers on p. 55. Carry the length over your arm and move on to the scaffold. Unfold the first fold and apply to the top of the wall. Be sure that your assistant takes the weight of the pasted paper, which will be quite considerable. Ask him to ease it down and to hold it away from the wall. If he lets it go suddenly it may well tear under the weight.

Now align your strip to the plumbed line in the usual way, trim the top while you have your scaffold at this level, and brush down the paper on to the wall as far as you can safely reach. Your assistant will help here, guiding the edge of the paper to the line and on to the wall. As he does so, you will be brushing out air pockets with your soft brush, having climbed down from your scaffold. Carry on hanging subsequent strips in the same way, adjusting your scaffolding to give maximum safety and working convenience. Each strip will get a little easier, owing to its decreasing length and lessening weight.

Try to allow an even amount of time between pasting and hanging each strip, because with the very long lengths some stretching may occur and, if you are using a paper that requires matching, you may find that your pattern will not accurately match up towards the bottom of the lengths. In this respect, the amateur would be well advised to consider the use of the new poly-ethylene papers, where the wall is pasted, not the paper (see p. 56). The increased ease of cutting, carrying and applying in the dry state has a great deal to recommend it for use on staircases.

New walls

Some new walls may not have had their plaster cured and sized. Unless they are sized you will find covering adhesion is poor, so, to be on the safe side, always size walls not previously covered with paper; it helps adhesion under any circumstances. The size seals the pores of new surfaces and stops the plaster breaking away if you want to strip the paper at some later date.

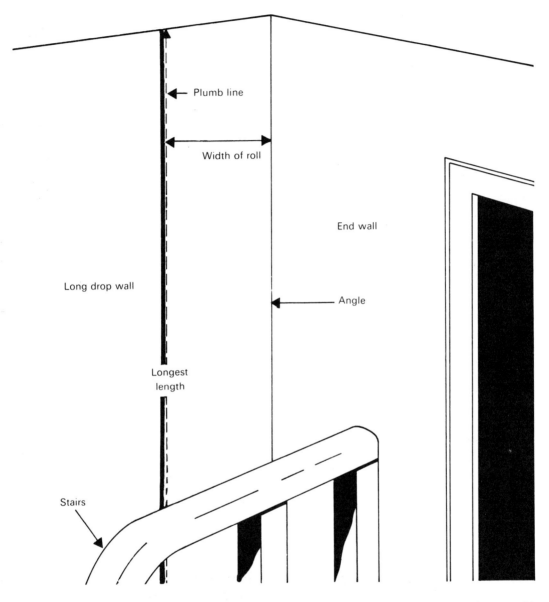

Plumb line

Width of roll

End wall

Long drop wall

Angle

Longest length

Stairs

Some walls are no more than plaster-board partitions. Such partitions need to be painted with an oil-based wall primer (see Chapter 3) before they can be successfully papered.

Finally, when you have hung your wall covering, sponge each strip down with water. Never use a rag for this job, it could leave marks. This final washing will remove any excess paste, dirt or finger marks. It also helps to keep the paper from wrinkling as the paste dries.

9 · Specialised Wall & Floor Coverings

Carpet tiles on the wall; vinyl tiles and panels. Floor and wall tiling. Simulated and genuine wooden finishes for walls. Armoured velvet.

Carpet tiles on walls

If you are an enthusiastic amateur rather than an 'of necessity' decorator, you will be looking for something a little different from the usual for your walls and special areas. This can arise from aesthetic or physical needs. For example, you may like to consider the use of carpet tiles for your walls in one room. Use of carpet tiles will provide texture, colour and a wide variety of patterns for a large wall. Perhaps you may decide to cover one wall only with tiles, the remainder being painted or covered in contrasting paper or vinyl. Carpet tiles are standardised at 300 mm (12 in.) square and are usually made of polypropylene olefin fibre, which is spot and stain-resistant. They can be used effectively in all rooms, including the bathroom, and are cleaned by normal vacuuming. They are very easy to lay and are resistant to action by damp and mould. Their comparatively small size makes them very easy to handle and cut to shape. A Stanley knife is ideal for cutting these tiles.

As a rule, these carpet tiles are not self-adhesive, so you should purchase the adhesive recommended by the manufacturers or advised by your supplier. They are made in a variety of colours and are usually textured in a definite direction so that, by tiling with alternate tiles at right-angles to one another, you can achieve an alternative textural appearance with no change of colour. Thus an almost infinite colour-texture pattern range can be achieved to choice. Although very effective on walls, they are equally attractive if used on floors, the purpose for which they were originally designed.

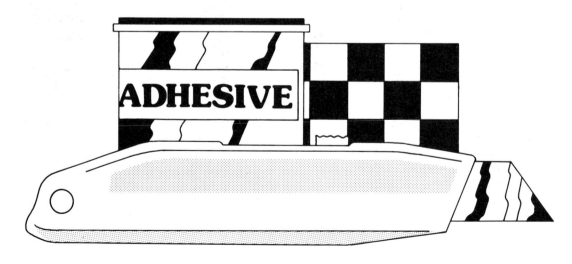

Vinyl tiles

Alternatively, you might prefer to use one of the modern 300 mm (12 in.) square pure vinyl tiles. These are very suitable for kitchen and bathroom floors and walls. They are easy to clean, scratch and stain-resistant and are quiet in use. Again, they are produced in a wide variety of colours, grains and patterns so that you can have a plain area, alternate coloured squares, patterned squares or any combination of all or any of these. The tiles are usually self-adhesive, requiring only that a backing strip be removed before applying the tile to the wall or floor.

A flat, well-finished but lightly textured surface must be provided as a base to receive the tiles and on no account must they be laid on a damp surface. Vinyl tiles, too, are easily and accurately cut with a Stanley knife, so that trimming around obstacles is quite an easy matter. On floors both types are ideal for use on areas of high stress and wear because the localised damage can be quickly, easily and cheaply repaired by changing round your squares or by replacing the seriously worn ones with the necessary number of new squares. Although a good flat surface is recommended for the laying of these tiles, they are so flexible that they will take up minor irregularities quite well.

Vinyl panels

A third possibility is the rigid vinyl panels that come in a variety of sizes, patterns and colours, while there are varieties that simulate stone and brick formations. These are very hard-wearing and are highly resistant to scratching, grease, stain and dirt. They are self-adhesive.

They are usually supplied in boxes in sufficient number to cover an area of about 1.1 sq m (12 sq ft.). Being rigid, they will require a little more skill and care, especially when being shaped around obstacles, and the surface will need to be that much flatter. They may be successfully cut with a fine-toothed saw and they can be filed.

For kitchens there are wall panels simulating wooden slats. These do require more expert fitting as they need to be applied to soft wood battens rawl-plugged to the wall. They are very durable, are easily cleaned by washing and can be aesthetically pleasing.

Ceramic tiles

Around wash-basins and kitchen sink areas, the ceramic tile is still the best solution for a clean, durable surface against practically any form of attack, scratching, staining or grease. The most popular sizes are 150 mm (6 in.) square or 100 mm (4 in.) square. They are produced in white and a variety of colours, usually pastel shades, and there is now a wide choice of patterned designs. The surface to which ceramic tiles are to be applied must be flat, dry, sound and free from cracks and holes. The latter should be filled and levelled with a good proprietary filler before tiling can commence (see p. 11). A special ceramic tile cement is needed to attach the tiles to the surface to be covered. This can be purchased quite cheaply from practically any hardware store and it comes in the form of a white powder, which is mixed with water. It is essential that the manufacturer's mixing instructions should be followed with great care.

Shaping the tiles

When shaping is required, tiles may be cut quite easily and accurately by using a tile cutter, purchased for a few pence from your local hardware store. The cutter is held against a straight-edge on the line required to be cut; it is then pressed hard against the tile and a deep scratch scored on the glazed side of the tile, coinciding with the marked line. The tile is then placed on a thin piece of wood, e.g. a piece of three-ply, a little larger all round than the tile, so that the scored line coincides with the edge of the wood. Downward pressure, by hand, is applied to the tile on the part overlapping the wood (see below) and the tile will snap cleanly along the scored line.

A tile cutter. The mild steel shank has a specially hardened tip to cut the tile. A plastic cap covers the tipped end when stored, and fits on the handle when in use

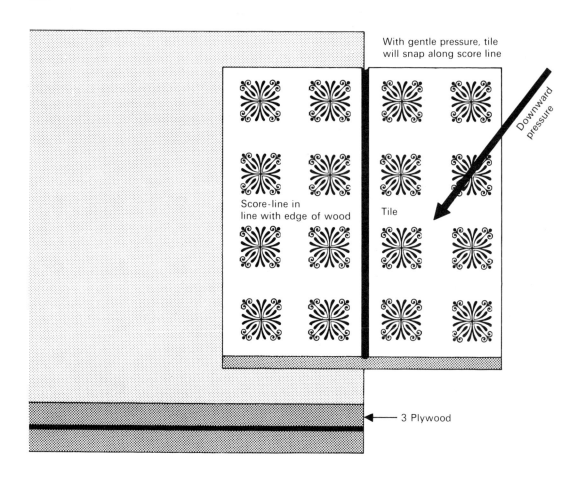

With gentle pressure, tile will snap along score line

Downward pressure

Score-line in line with edge of wood

Tile

3 Plywood

Tile cement being 'keyed' in a criss-cross pattern by a plastic comb. Note how the tiles are being built up from the bottom of the area to be covered

Fixing the tiles

To fix your tiles, you should apply sufficient cement to cover about 0.2 sq m (2 sq ft.). Use a small, wet trowel for this work. The cement should then be combed out with a plastic comb (see above) that will be supplied with the cement. Make sure that the teeth of the comb cut right through the cement to the original surface. Then press the tiles into position, starting with the bottom ones, to avoid 'sinking' on the wet cement, and leave for two hours to dry. The small spaces left between the tiles should then be filled in with a white 'grout', purchased from the same dealer, to give a smooth and even finish.

Tile patterns

If you are tiling a vertical surface, start at the bottom and build up. There are two ways of arranging the pattern of your tiles:

- With all vertical joint lines in one continuous line; this is the current modern trend.
- With the joint lines of alternate horizontal rows being 'staggered' by half the

width of a tile (shown below). This is the older method which has the advantage of eliminating a line of weakness in the joint, each tile being supported by the two below it.

Alternative arrangements for joint lines in tiling

Continuous vertical joint lines

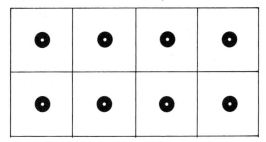

Staggered joint lines

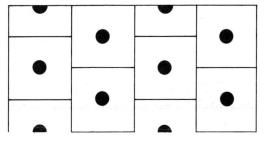

When tiles are adjacent to edges, round-edged tiles should be used; one edge rounded for horizontal and vertical edges and two edges rounded when the tile is used on a corner. These round-edged tiles provide a smooth, finished appearance and eliminate the sharp, possibly dangerous, edge that would otherwise be present.

Wooden finishes to walls

This is the 'ultimate' in wall finishes. Ideal for kitchens and attractive in its varying forms for other rooms, this finish requires that the operator shall have rather more skill, experience and equipment than he would need for the finishes described earlier. It is not, however, beyond the ability of a good DIY enthusiast, handy with tools and possessed of patience and determination. The wood available to the home decorator divides into two main types:

Hardwood of which cedar is probably the best, although beech, if available, is a very clean, pleasant wood.

Softwood which, for the purposes we are discussing, will be basically pine or fir.

Buying the wood

You will need to purchase specially prepared timber for this work, with tongued and grooved edges to allow for natural expansion and shrinkage (see below), especially if used on kitchen walls; consult your local timber merchant and go on his advice. Softwoods are usually marketed by the foot run (length) or by the metre (tongued and grooved boards are 100–150 mm wide), while hardwoods are usually marketed by the square foot or square metre. Measure your walls and give the sizes to your supplier; he will then let you know how much timber you require, but be sure to give him the *height* of your room so that, for the sake of economy, multiples of that length can be supplied to you, eliminating a whole lot of short ends that total up to a great deal of wasted wood. No timber is cheap these days but, in general, softwoods are usually cheaper than hardwoods.

Battening the wall

You will need to batten your walls to receive the planking. This is best done by using 50 mm × 18 mm (2 in. × $\frac{3}{4}$ in.) ready-planed softwood. This will probably be 50 mm × 18 mm Russian red deal; watch out for large knots that could weaken your battens and refuse any wood that is seriously twisted. You should use cross-halving joints and 'T' halving joints (see opposite) for your battening and these should be glued and screwed together. The frame should be rawl-plugged to the wall. Your frame should provide a series of 50 mm × 50 mm (2 in. × 2 in.) squares all over the area to be covered by the boards. When the frame is in place, cut your timber to the precise size that you require, cutting all the full lengths first. Now, using the grooved edge of one board, start to attach it to the frame on, say, the left-hand corner of your room or area, making sure that the flat edge of the board is hard up to the corner. If the wall abutting the

Cross-section of a wall-board, showing the grooved and tongued edges

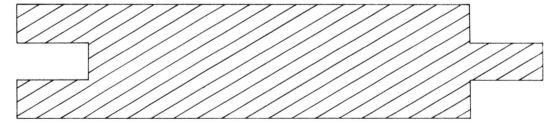

edge is not true, you will have to shape the edge of the board to fit the contour of the wall by using a small smoothing plane or a Surform tool. The fit of this first board is the key to a successful covering, since the long vertical joints between the boards emphasise any out-of-vertical edges.

Wall battening to receive decorative planking

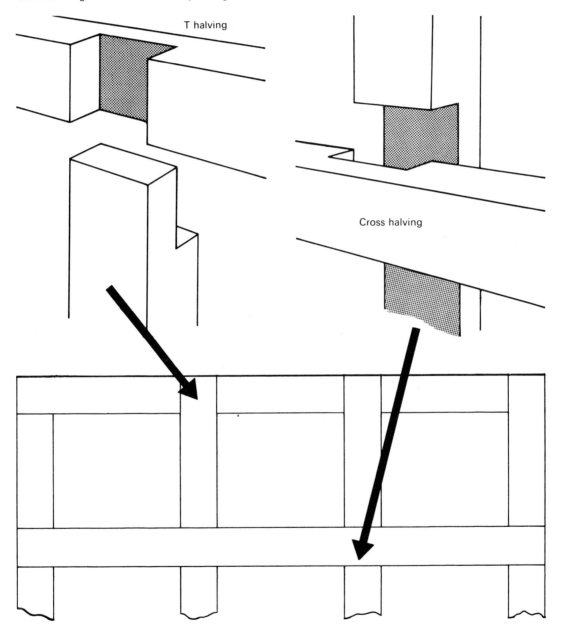

T halving

Cross halving

Pinning the wood to the wall

Using 40 mm (1½ in.) panel pins, pin the board to the horizontal battens behind it, having marked the location of these battens in chalk on the face of the board. These panel pins are the only ones that might show a little if you do not punch them below the surface of the wood with a pin punch and then fill the small hole with matching wood filler. They should be about 25 mm (1 in.) in from the edge nearest the corner from which you started.

Now, using 25 mm (1 in.) panel pins, attach the other, right-hand edge of the board to the framing by driving the pins through the tongue, close up to the board and at a slight angle, so that they do not come out on the underside of the tongue and obstruct the fit of the second board, and then punch the head of the pin just below the surface of the tongue. When the second board is offered up to the first board and the tongue of the latter fits into the groove of the former, the panel pins will become invisible and will be sufficient to hold the second board in place down its left-hand edge. Treat the right-hand edge of the second board in the same way as the first and proceed in this way until you have finished the whole area. The right-hand edge of the final board will have to be sawn and planed flat or shaped to the adjacent corner in the same way as the first board had to be shaped on its left-hand edge. It will then have to be pinned, with 40 mm (1½ in.) panel pins, as was the first board, the pin heads being punched below the surface of the wood and the resulting depression filled with matching wood-filler.

Finishing the surface

Softwood panelling should, after fitting, be lightly glass-papered all over, in the direction of the grain, using grade F1 on a block of wood. This will remove any working marks, grease and surface roughness. You should then apply one coat of thinned, polyurethane varnish to act as a sealer. When this coat has thoroughly dried, again rub lightly down with glass-paper (grade F1) and apply a further two coats of polyurethane varnish (unthinned this time). Allow at least, eight hours between coats and rub down with No. 0 glass-paper between these final coats. You can use either glossy or satin finish varnish, to your own taste.

If you use cedar, you should use a cedar dressing instead of varnish. Alternative hardwoods, such as beech, should be varnished or hard-wax polished. Areas finished in wood in this way are extremely durable and only require to be washed down and very lightly glass-papered every two or three years and given a further coat of varnish or dressing.

Armoured velvet

There are other wall finishes, such as armoured velvet, which provides a measure of sound damping and thermal insulation. It comes in an attractive range of colours and, to many, is aesthetically very pleasing. Armoured velvet may be applied to practically any type of surface, including metal, wood, glass, plastic and even masonry. It is dirt-resistant and is normally cleaned by vacuuming. It is fire-resistant, and resists mould and most stains. There are two drawbacks to its general use; it cannot be applied by the amateur decorator and it is by far the most expensive covering on the market, but for a really outstanding effect, the home owner might feel he could run to one wall being treated in this way, completing the other walls in contrasting cover in any of the ways described above.

This book does not exhaust the possibilities open to the amateur home decorator; but its aim has been to explain the merits and uses of a wide variety of internal and external finishes which come within the range of the average householder's ability. Experience and enthusiasm will decide how much further you want to go. Below are a helpful bibliography and names of resources. Many of the books named will take the keen amateur a step farther into specialist fields, but I am sure the majority will be more than satisfied to achieve success within the practical limits covered here.

Bibliography & Resources

Dampness in Buildings, R. T. Gratwick (Crosby Lockwood, 1975)
Home Decorating, Victor John Taylor (Barker, 1971)
Home Electrical Repairs, L. Wakelin (EP Publishing Ltd, 1977)
Basic Woodworking, R. W. Draycon (EP Publishing Ltd, 1977)
House Decoration, A. V. Lovegrove (Evans Bros)
Floors and their Maintenance, J. K. P. Edwards (Butterworth, 1972)
Money Saving Home Maintenance, H. H. Cobb (Macmillan)
Let's Decorate, Roy Day (I.C.I. Ltd)
Painting and Decorating, A. E. Hurst (Griffin, 1963)
Painting and Decorating, L. F. J. Tubb (Macmillan, 1974)
Painting and Wallpapering, Leanna Landsmann (Grosset & Dunlap)
Painter & Decorator's Book of Facts, J. Snelling (Technical Press Ltd, 1972)
Practical Guide to Paperhanging, L. Sheppard (S. Paul)
The Practical Handbook of Painting and Wallpapering, Morton Schultz (W. Foulsham & Co, 1973)

Resources

I.C.I. Advisory Service	London W1A 3AU
Dulux Specifiers Manual	Published by the Dulux Trade Group
	Imperial Chemical Industries Ltd
	London Sales Office
	PO Box 19, Templar House
	81–87 High Holborn
	London WC1V 6NP

Glossary

Abrasion: The wearing away of a paint film by a mechanical abrasive.

Acrylic: A monomer or polymer (q.v.) which has the attributes of colour fastness, long-lasting gloss and excellent all-round durability.

Alkali: The opposite of an acid, which it has the power to neutralise. Alkalis are soluble salts and they are called 'bases'.

Alkyd: A chemical combination of acid, oil and alcohol. It is a common vehicle for paint.

Base: A thick liquid or paste which is added to paint in order to tint it. Finished paint is the product of a base to which a vehicle has been added.

Batten: A strip of wood which, for its length, is of comparatively small section, e.g. 3 m × 50 mm × 18 mm (10 ft. × 2 in. × $\frac{3}{4}$ in.).

Binder: This is a vehicle solid, more often than not a polymer (q.v.) and is the part of a paint which holds the pigment particles together.

Cellulose: A natural polymer (q.v.), usually of wood or cotton.

Coverage: The area a given volume of paint will cover at a stated thickness.

Crazing: This is where the surface of a paint film breaks up into a large number of fine cracks.

Curing: This is where paints dry by means of a chemical reaction, resulting in a chemical change in the paint.

Drier: A paint additive which increases the speed of drying.

Emulsion: A suspension of polymer (q.v.) particles in a liquid.

Enamel: A form of pigmented gloss paint giving a hard finish. Usually comparatively quick drying.

Facia (Fascia) Boards: A flat board used to cover a joint or to provide a decorative band of colour or texture.

Flaking: As applied to paint, this means areas of the paint breaking away from the surface to which it has been applied.

Flat: Having little or no shine or gloss.

Flow: The power of a paint film to level out evenly.

Fungicide: A substance added to paint to increase its resistance to attack by mould or fungi.

Gloss: Describes the ability of a painted surface to reflect light, giving a high shine appearance.

Haze: A semi-opaque misting over on a film of paint or in a clear liquid.

Holiday: A part of a surface not covered by paint when it should have been.

Inhibitor: A substance added to a paint which retards certain processes such as speed of drying, yellowing or the development of skin.

Key: A textured or slightly roughened surface provides a 'key' or 'grip' in order to hold an adhesive or to provide a required amount of friction on a surface.

Latex: An emulsion. A dispersion of a polymer (q.v.) in water.

Lifting: The breaking away of a finishing coat of paint from its undercoat as a result of interacting solvents.

Linseed Oil: A vegetable oil used in the production of alkyd resins. It is also used as a binder on its own account.

Mastic: A semi-fluid, usually waterproof, flexible filler for joints, crevices and cracks. Used widely for eliminating dampness, it is, basically, bitumastic in content.

Mildew: A formation of mould on the surface of a variety of materials, encouraged by warm, damp conditions.

Monomer: Basically, a simple chemical compound, capable of reacting with itself or other monomers (q.v.) to form polymers (q.v.). Vinyl acetate is a monomer.

Pointing: The process of 'neatening-up' the mortar in the gap between two rows of bricks by using a smoother 'mix' and trowelling it more carefully. All brickwork on houses is treated in this way.

Polymer: The chemical combination of a chain of units formed from monomers (q.v.) by polymerisation. Polyvinyl acetate, for example, is a polymer formed by the linking together of many vinyl acetate units.

Polymerisation: The process of changing the molecular arrangement of a compound so as to form new compounds having the same percentage composition as the original, but of different molecular weight and different properties. The resulting molecular weight is usually greater.

Primer: The initial coat of paint applied to any surface. It plays an important part in controlling corrosion, blistering and loss of adhesion.

Resin: The film-forming constituent in paint.

Retarder: A solvent which is added to paint to slow down the rate of evaporation or drying out.

Sagging: The result of too thick a coat of paint. This gives rise to 'runs', drips and 'curtaining' of the painted surface.

Sanding: The cleaning and smoothing of a surface by rubbing with an abrasive material such as glass-paper. Can refer to a mechanical process to produce the same result on a large scale.

Sheen: The surface reflection of a film when viewed from a low angle.

Size: A thin solution of glue, adhesive or paste used to 'prime' a surface so that anything to be stuck to it will adhere more securely.

Skinning: The development of a solid film over the surface of standing paint in a container.

Stabiliser: A substance added to a paint to prevent deterioration.

Straight-edge: A perfectly straight strip of wood or metal, 750 mm–1 m (29–39 in.) long. Used for drawing straight lines or for use as a 'fence' when cutting to a line with, say, a Stanley knife.

Thinner: A solvent used to reduce the viscosity of paint, i.e. to make it thinner.

Undercoat: A non-gloss coat of paint performing the function of a sealer or primer. It provides an ideal surface to receive a finishing coat.

Varnish: A clear, almost colourless, liquid produced by the action of heat on hard gum and vegetable oil. The product thus formed is then dissolved in an organic solvent. Ideal for use on floors, doors, etc., when a gloss finish is required, particularly in circumstances where the natural grain of the wood is required to be seen.

Vinyl: A group of monomers combined to form vinyl polymers which are flexible, durable and hard-wearing.

Viscosity: The fluidity of a liquid; particularly characterised by its resistance to flow. Water has a low viscosity but thick oil (E.P.90) would have a high viscosity.

Wrinkling: A clearly defined pattern in the surface film of a paint, usually caused by excessively heavy coats, commonly appearing as raised lines, folds or ridges.

Zinc chromate: A rust-resistant pigment, useful on ferrous metals.

Zinc oxide: Used to prevent mildew or mould on paint film.